Macmillan McGraw-Hill

Math Connects

5

Chapter 10
Resource Masters

Mc Graw Hill Macmillan/McGraw-Hill

The *McGraw·Hill* Companies

 Macmillan/McGraw-Hill

Copyright © by The McGraw-Hill Companies, Inc. All rights reserved. Permission is
granted to reproduce the material contained herein on the condition that such materials
be reproduced only for classroom use; be provided to students, teachers, and families
without charge; and be used solely in conjunction with the *Math Connects* program.
Any other reproduction, for sale or other use, is expressly prohibited.

Send all inquiries to:
Macmillan/McGraw-Hill
8787 Orion Place
Columbus, OH 43240-4027

ISBN: 978-0-02-107282-8
MHID: 0-02-107282-5

Chapter 10 Resource Masters

Printed in the United States of America.

4 5 6 7 8 9 10 RHR 16 15 14 13 12 11 10 09

CONTENTS

Teacher's Guide to Using the
Chapter 10 Resource Masters

The *Chapter 10 Resource Masters* includes the core materials needed for Chapter 10. These materials include worksheets, extensions, and assessment options. The answers for these pages appear at the back of this booklet.

All of the materials found in this booklet are included for viewing and printing on the *TeacherWorks Plus*™ CD-ROM.

Chapter Resources

Graphic Organizer (page 1) This master is a tool designed to assist students with comprehension of grade-level concepts. While the content and layout of these tools vary, their goal is to assist students by providing a visual representation from which they can learn new concepts.

Student Glossary (page 2) This master is a study tool that presents the key vocabulary terms from the chapter. You may suggest that students highlight or star the terms they do not understand. Give this list to students before beginning Lesson 10–1. Remind them to add these pages to their mathematics study notebooks.

Anticipation Guide (page 6) This master is a survey designed for use before beginning the chapter. You can use this survey to highlight what students may or may not know about the concepts in the chapter. There is space for recording how well students answer the questions before they complete the chapter. You may find it helpful to interview students a second time, after completing the chapter, to determine their progress.

Game (page 7) A game is provided to reinforce chapter concepts and may be used at appropriate times throughout the chapter.

Resources for Computational Lessons

Reteach Each lesson has an associated Reteach worksheet. In general, the Reteach worksheet focuses on the same lesson content but uses a different approach, learning style, or modality than that used in the Student Edition. The Reteach worksheet closes with computational practice of the concept.

Skills Practice The Skills Practice worksheet for each lesson focuses on the computational aspect of the lesson. The Skills Practice worksheet may be helpful in providing additional practice of the skill taught in the lesson.

Homework Practice The Homework Practice worksheet provides an opportunity for additional computational practice. The Homework Practice worksheet includes word problems that address the skill taught in the lesson.

Problem-Solving Practice The Problem-Solving Practice worksheet presents additional reinforcement in solving word problems that apply both the concepts of the lesson and some review concepts.

Enrich The Enrich worksheet presents activities that extend the concepts of the lesson. Some Enrich materials are designed to widen students' perspectives on the mathematics they are learning. These worksheets are written for use with all levels of students.

Resources for Problem-Solving Strategy and Problem-Solving Investigation Lessons In recognition of the importance of problem-solving strategies, worksheets for problem-solving lessons follow a slightly different format. For problem-solving lessons, a two-page Reteach worksheet offers a complete model for choosing a problem-solving strategy. For each Problem-Solving Strategy lesson, Reteach and Homework Practice worksheets offer reinforcement of the strategy taught in the Student Edition lesson. In contrast, the Problem-Solving

Investigation worksheets include a model strategy on the Reteach worksheets and provide problems requiring several alternate strategies on the Homework Practice and Skills Practice worksheets.

Assessment Options The assessment masters in the *Chapter 10 Resource Masters* offer a wide variety of assessment tools for monitoring progress as well as final assessment.

Individual Progress Checklist This checklist explains the chapter's goals or objectives. Teachers can record whether a student's mastery of each objective is beginning (B), developing (D), or mastered (M). The checklist includes space to record notes to parents as well as other pertinent observations.

Chapter Diagnostic Test This one-page test assesses students' grasp of skills that are needed for success in the chapter.

Chapter Pretest This one-page quick check of the chapter's concepts is useful for determining pacing. Performance on the pretest can help you determine which concepts can be covered quickly and which specific concepts may need additional time.

Mid-Chapter Test This one-page chapter test provides an option to assess the first half of the chapter. It includes both multiple-choice and free-response questions.

Quizzes Three free-response quizzes offer quick assessment opportunities at appropriate intervals in the chapter.

Vocabulary Test This one-page test focuses on chapter vocabulary. It is suitable for all students. It includes a list of vocabulary words and questions to assess students' knowledge of the words.

Oral Assessment This two-page test consists of one page for teacher directions and questions and a second page for recording responses. Although this assessment is designed to be used with all students, the interview format focuses on assessing chapter content assimilated by ELL students.

Chapter Project Rubric This one-page rubric is designed for use in assessing the chapter project. You may want to distribute copies of the rubric when you assign the project and use the rubric to record each student's chapter project score.

Foldables Rubric This one-page rubric is designed to assess the Foldables graphic organizer. The rubric is written to the students, telling them what you will be looking for as you evaluate their completed Foldables graphic organizer.

Leveled Chapter Tests

- **Form 1** assesses basic chapter concepts through multiple-choice questions and is designed for use with on-level students.

- **Form 2A** is designed for on-level students and is primarily for those who may have missed the Form 1 test. It may be used as a retest for students who received additional instruction following the Form 1 test.

- **Form 2B** is designed for students with a below-level command of the English language.

- **Form 2C** is a free-response test designed for on-level students.

- **Form 2D** is written for students with a below-level command of the English language.

- **Form 3** is a free-response test written for above-level students.

- **Extended-Response Test** is an extended response test for on-level students.

Cumulative Standardized Test Practice This three-page test, aimed at on-level students, offers multiple-choice questions and free-response questions.

Student Recording Sheet This one-page recording sheet is for the standardized test in the Student Edition.

Answers

The answers for the Anticipation Guide and Lesson Resources are provided as reduced pages with answers appearing in black. Full size line-up answer keys are provided for the Assessment Masters.

Use this graphic organizer to take notes on **Chapter 10: Add and Subtract Fractions**. Fill in the missing information.

Adding and Subtracting Like Fractions

○○○●● + ○○○○● =	Like fractions have the same _____. Are these like fractions? Y or N What is the total of the two fractions?
$\dfrac{2}{3} - \dfrac{1}{3} =$	
If there are 8 apples altogether and one person eats 2 apples and another eats 1, how many of the 8 are left? How would you show this situation in an equation?	
$\dfrac{3}{4} - \dfrac{1}{4} =$	Is this fraction in its simplest form? Y or N If not, what is the simplified fraction?

Name _____ Date _____

Student-Built Glossary

This is an alphabetical list of new vocabulary terms you will learn in **Chapter 10: Model Adding and Subtracting Fractions**. As you study the chapter, complete each term's definition or description. Remember to add the page number where you found the term. Add this page to your math study notebook to review vocabulary at the end of the chapter.

Vocabulary Term	Found on Page	Definition/Description/Example
denominator		
improper fraction		
like fractions		
numerator		
simplest form		
unlike fraction		

Dear Family,

Today my class started **Chapter 10: Add and Subtract Fractions.** I will be learning to add and subtract fractions. I will also be learning to estimate sums and differences of mixed numbers. Additionally, I will solve problems by determining reasonable answers. Here are my vocabulary words and an activity we can do together.

Sincerely, _____

Key Vocabulary

like fractions: Fractions that have the same denominator.

numerator: The part of the fraction that tells how many of the equal parts are being used.

denominator: The bottom number in a fraction.

improper fraction: A number in which the numerator is greater than the denominator.

simplest form: The form of a fraction when the GCF of the numerator and the denominator is one.

unlike fractions: Fraction that have different denominators.

Activity

Examples of fractions are everywhere! Make a list of all the different places where you might find fractions. Write down three examples, along with addition and subtraction sentences to represent them.

Books to Read

Pizza Counting
by Christina Dobson

The Fraction Family Moves West
by Marti Dryk

Gator Pie
by Louise Mathews

MATEMÁTICAS en CASA

Estimada familia:

Hoy mi clase comenzó el **Capítulo 10, Suma y resta fracciones.**
Aprenderé a estimar sumas y diferencias de números mixtos. También
aprenderé a estimar sumas y diferencias de números mixtos. Además,
resolveré problemas usando la estrategia de elegir el método de
cálculo. A continuación, están mis palabras del vocabulario y una
actividad que podemos realizar juntos.

Sinceramente, _____

Vocabulario clave

fracciones semejantes: Fracciones con el
mismo denominador.

numerador: La parte de la fracción que indica
cuántas de las partes iguales se están usando.

denominador: El número inferior en una
fracción.

fracción impropia: Número en el cual el
numerador es mayor que el denominador.

forma reducida: Forma de una fracción cuando
el MCD del numerador y del denominador es
uno.

fracciones desiguales:
Fracciones que tienen
distintos denominadores.

Actividad

Ejemplos de fracciones se
encuentran por doquier. Hagan
una lista de todos los distintos
lugares donde podrían encontrar
fracciones. Escriban tres ejemplos,
junto con oraciones de suma y
resta para representarlas.

Libros recomendados

Pizza Counting (Conteo de pizza)
de Christina Dobson

**The Fraction Family Moves West
(La familia Fracción se muda al oeste)**
de Marti Dryk

Gator Pie (Pastel de cocodrilo)
de Louise Mathews

10

Anticipation Guide

Add and Subtract Fractions

STEP 1   ***Before you begin Chapter 10***

- Read each statement.

- Decide whether you agree (A) or disagree (D) with the statement.

- Write A or D in the first column OR if you are not sure whether you agree or disagree, write NS (not sure).

STEP 1 A, D, or NS	Statement	STEP 2 A or D
	1. Like fractions have the same denominator.	
	2. Unlike fractions have the same numerator.	
	3. $\frac{1}{7}$ and $\frac{6}{7}$ are like fractions.	
	4. $\frac{13}{4}$ is a mixed number.	
	5. $2\frac{1}{2}$ is an improper fraction.	

STEP 2   ***After you complete Chapter 10***

- Reread each statement and complete the last column by entering an A (agree) or a D (disagree).

- Did any of your opinions about the statements change from the first column?

- For those statements that you mark with a D, use a separate sheet of paper to explain why you disagree. Use examples, if possible.

10

Game

Add it all up!

Ready

- 4 number cubes
- Paper and pencil

Set

Give each player paper and a pencil.

GO!

1. Have the first player toss all 4 cubes and create 2 fractions from the 4 cubes. For example, if a 3, 4, 5, and 6 are tossed, the fractions could be $\frac{3}{4}$ and $\frac{5}{6}$, or $\frac{5}{4}$ and $\frac{3}{6}$, etc.

2. Add the 2 fractions together.

3. Have the other players toss the cubes, create fractions, and add their fractions together. That is the player's score for the round.

4. Repeat the steps, adding together the scores from each round. The first player to reach a total of 20 wins the game.

Name _____ Date _____

Reteach

Add Like Fractions

Follow these steps to add fractions with like denominators.

Add $\frac{3}{8} + \frac{1}{8}$

Step 1

Add the numerators.
Use the like denominator.

$\frac{3}{8} + \frac{1}{8} = \frac{4}{8}$

So, $\frac{3}{8} + \frac{1}{8} = \frac{4}{8}$.

Step 2

Write the sum in simplest form.
Divide the numerator and denominator
by their greatest common factor.

$$\frac{4}{8} = \frac{4 \div 4}{8 \div 4} = \frac{1}{2}$$

Add. Write each sum in simplest form.

1. $\frac{5}{7} + \frac{4}{7} =$ _____

2. $\frac{1}{4} + \frac{1}{4} =$ _____

3. $\frac{3}{10} + \frac{1}{10} =$ _____

4. $\frac{7}{8} + \frac{5}{8} =$ _____

5. $\frac{11}{12} + \frac{7}{12} =$ _____

6. $\frac{3}{10} + \frac{2}{10} =$ _____

7. $\frac{1}{3} + \frac{3}{3} =$ _____

8. $\frac{1}{2} + \frac{3}{2} =$ _____

9. $\frac{1}{9} + \frac{3}{9} =$ _____

10. $\frac{1}{7} + \frac{4}{7} =$ _____

11. $\frac{2}{10} + \frac{3}{10} =$ _____

12. $\frac{1}{6} + \frac{3}{6} =$ _____

Name _____ Date _____

Skills Practice

Add Like Fractions

Add. Write each in simplest form.

1. $\dfrac{7}{10} + \dfrac{1}{10} =$ _____

2. $\dfrac{13}{16} + \dfrac{7}{16} =$ _____

3. $\dfrac{4}{5} + \dfrac{1}{5} =$ _____

4. $\dfrac{7}{12} + \dfrac{5}{12} =$ _____

5. $\dfrac{4}{5} + \dfrac{3}{5} =$ _____

6. $\dfrac{5}{6} + \dfrac{5}{6} =$ _____

7. $\dfrac{7}{15} + \dfrac{2}{15} =$ _____

8. $\dfrac{9}{20} + \dfrac{3}{20} =$ _____

9. $\dfrac{1}{4} + \dfrac{1}{4} =$ _____

10. $\dfrac{3}{8} + \dfrac{1}{8} =$ _____

11. $\dfrac{2}{3} + \dfrac{1}{3} =$ _____

12. $\dfrac{5}{6} + \dfrac{1}{6} =$ _____

13. $\dfrac{7}{16} + \dfrac{3}{16} =$ _____

14. $\dfrac{3}{10} + \dfrac{9}{10} =$ _____

15. $\dfrac{7}{8} + \dfrac{7}{8} =$ _____

16. $\dfrac{7}{12} + \dfrac{11}{12} =$ _____

17. $\dfrac{19}{20} + \dfrac{5}{20} =$ _____

18. $\dfrac{11}{20} + \dfrac{7}{20} =$ _____

19. $\dfrac{9}{16} + \dfrac{7}{16} =$ _____

20. $\dfrac{4}{5} + \dfrac{3}{5} =$ _____

21. $\dfrac{7}{9} + \dfrac{4}{9} =$ _____

Replace each ◯ with >, <, or = to make a true sentence.

22. $\dfrac{7}{8} + \dfrac{5}{8}$ ◯ $\dfrac{3}{4} + \dfrac{3}{4}$

23. $\dfrac{7}{10} + \dfrac{9}{10}$ ◯ $\dfrac{3}{5} + \dfrac{4}{5}$

24. $\dfrac{2}{3} + \dfrac{2}{3}$ ◯ $\dfrac{5}{12} + \dfrac{7}{12}$

25. $\dfrac{3}{8} + \dfrac{3}{8}$ ◯ $\dfrac{9}{16} + \dfrac{5}{16}$

26. $\dfrac{3}{5} + \dfrac{3}{5}$ ◯ $\dfrac{7}{10} + \dfrac{7}{10}$

27. $\dfrac{5}{8} + \dfrac{7}{8}$ ◯ $\dfrac{13}{16} + \dfrac{11}{16}$

Name _____ Date _____

Homework Practice

Add Like Fractions

Add. Write each sum in simplest form.

1. $\frac{2}{5} + \frac{8}{5} =$ _____

2. $\frac{5}{9} + \frac{1}{9} =$ _____

3. $\frac{6}{8} + \frac{5}{8} =$ _____

4. $\frac{3}{4} + \frac{2}{4} =$ _____

5. $\frac{9}{9} + \frac{3}{9} =$ _____

6. $\frac{7}{8} + \frac{2}{8} =$ _____

7. $\frac{1}{2} + \frac{2}{2} =$ _____

8. $\frac{4}{5} + \frac{3}{5} =$ _____

9. $\frac{12}{15} + \frac{3}{15} =$ _____

10. $\frac{6}{7} + \frac{1}{7} =$ _____

11. Jasmine ate $\frac{3}{8}$ of a pizza. Manny ate $\frac{2}{8}$ of the same pizza. How much pizza did they eat altogether? Write a fraction in simplest form.

12. Deanna walked $\frac{4}{15}$ of a mile. Abi walked $\frac{5}{15}$ of a mile. How far did they walk altogether? Write as a fraction in simplest form.

_____

_____

Spiral Review

Replace each ◯ with <, >, or = to make a true statement. (Lesson 9–9)

13. $\frac{1}{4}$ ◯ $\frac{3}{8}$

14. $\frac{2}{3}$ ◯ $\frac{6}{9}$

15. $\frac{1}{2}$ ◯ $\frac{5}{9}$

16. $\frac{1}{5}$ ◯ $\frac{2}{7}$

17. $\frac{3}{4}$ ◯ $\frac{5}{8}$

18. $\frac{7}{12}$ ◯ $\frac{6}{13}$

Name _____ Date _____

Problem-Solving Practice

Add Like Fractions

Solve. Write your answer in simplest form.

1. Debbie helped her mother with the laundry. She did $\frac{1}{8}$ of it on Monday and another $\frac{3}{8}$ of it on Tuesday. What fraction of the laundry has she done?

_____

2. Laureano worked $\frac{1}{4}$ hour one day and $\frac{3}{4}$ hour the next day. How many hours did he work on the two days?

_____

3. Mindy likes to order fresh meat and vegetable wraps from a local restaurant. One cook can roll $\frac{1}{3}$ wraps in 5 minutes. Another cook can roll $\frac{2}{3}$ wraps in the same amount of time. How many wraps can the two cooks prepare in 5 minutes?

_____

4. John went to a museum to see model trains. He saw $\frac{2}{5}$ mile of track on the first floor of the museum. He saw $\frac{4}{5}$ mile of track on the second floor. How much track did John see?

_____

5. Sherry was in charge of distributing 250 food items that were donated to the local food pantry. On Monday she distributed 87 items. On Tuesday, she distributed 63 more items. Fifty more items were distributed on Wednesday. What fraction of the food items was distributed by the end of the day on Wednesday?

_____

6. Laura and her sister Katie swim every day. Laura can swim $\frac{3}{7}$ mile in 10 minutes. Katie can swim $\frac{2}{7}$ mile in the same amount of time. If they swim for 20 minutes and their speeds stay the same, how far do the sisters swim?

_____

Chapter Resources

Name _____ Date _____

Enrich

Fraction Pyramid!

In this triangle, the number in each blank circle is equal to the sum of
the fractions in the two circles above it.

Add to find the missing fractions to complete the triangle.
Do not write your answers in simplest form.

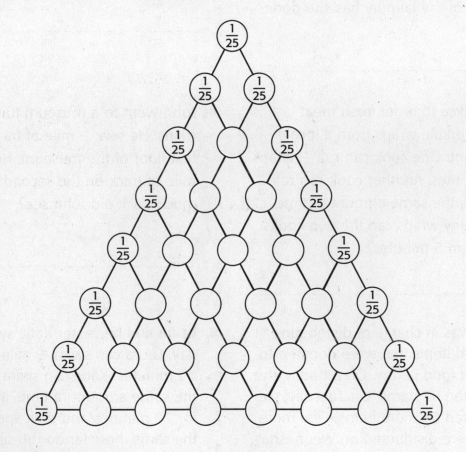

How many fractions less than 1 can you simplify in the triangle? _____

Write the fractions in simplest form. _____

How many fractions in the triangle are greater than 1? _____

Write the fractions in simplest form. _____

Name _____ Date _____

Reteach

Subtract Like Fractions

Follow these steps to subtract fractions with like denominators.

Subtract $\dfrac{8}{9} - \dfrac{2}{9}$

Step 1

Subtract the numerators.
Use the like denominator.

$$\dfrac{8}{9} - \dfrac{2}{9} = \dfrac{6}{9}$$

So, $\dfrac{8}{9} - \dfrac{2}{9} = \dfrac{6}{9} = \dfrac{2}{3}$.

Step 2

Write the difference in simplest form.
Divide the numerator and denominator by
their greatest common factor.

$$\dfrac{6}{9} = \dfrac{6 \div 3}{9 \div 3} = \dfrac{2}{3}$$

Subtract. Write each difference in simplest form.

1. $\dfrac{5}{7} - \dfrac{4}{7} =$ _____

2. $\dfrac{3}{4} - \dfrac{1}{4} =$ _____

3. $\dfrac{3}{10} - \dfrac{1}{10} =$ _____

4. $\dfrac{7}{8} - \dfrac{5}{8} =$ _____

5. $\dfrac{11}{12} - \dfrac{7}{12} =$ _____

6. $\dfrac{3}{10} - \dfrac{2}{10} =$ _____

7. $\dfrac{4}{6} - \dfrac{1}{6} =$ _____

8. $\dfrac{4}{3} - \dfrac{2}{3} =$ _____

9. $\dfrac{12}{9} - \dfrac{4}{9} =$ _____

10. $\dfrac{3}{2} - \dfrac{2}{2} =$ _____

11. $\dfrac{7}{8} - \dfrac{1}{8} =$ _____

12. $\dfrac{10}{10} - \dfrac{4}{10} =$ _____

Name _____ Date _____

Skills Practice

Subtract Like Fractions

Subtract. Write each difference in simplest form.

1. $\dfrac{7}{10} - \dfrac{1}{10} =$ _____

2. $\dfrac{13}{16} - \dfrac{7}{16} =$ _____

3. $\dfrac{4}{5} - \dfrac{1}{5} =$ _____

4. $\dfrac{7}{12} - \dfrac{5}{12} =$ _____

5. $\dfrac{4}{5} - \dfrac{3}{5} =$ _____

6. $\dfrac{5}{6} - \dfrac{4}{6} =$ _____

7. $\dfrac{7}{15} - \dfrac{2}{15} =$ _____

8. $\dfrac{9}{20} - \dfrac{3}{20} =$ _____

9. $\dfrac{3}{8} - \dfrac{1}{8} =$ _____

10. $\dfrac{3}{8} - \dfrac{1}{8} =$ _____

11. $\dfrac{2}{3} - \dfrac{1}{3} =$ _____

12. $\dfrac{5}{6} - \dfrac{1}{6} =$ _____

13. $\dfrac{7}{16} - \dfrac{3}{16} =$ _____

14. $\dfrac{9}{10} - \dfrac{3}{10} =$ _____

15. $\dfrac{7}{8} - \dfrac{7}{8} =$ _____

16. $\dfrac{11}{12} - \dfrac{7}{12} =$ _____

17. $\dfrac{19}{20} - \dfrac{5}{20} =$ _____

18. $\dfrac{11}{20} - \dfrac{7}{20} =$ _____

19. $\dfrac{9}{16} - \dfrac{7}{16} =$ _____

20. $\dfrac{4}{5} - \dfrac{3}{5} =$ _____

Replace each ◯ with >, <, or = to make a true sentence.

21. $\dfrac{7}{8} - \dfrac{5}{8}$ ◯ $\dfrac{3}{4} - \dfrac{3}{4}$

22. $\dfrac{9}{10} - \dfrac{7}{10}$ ◯ $\dfrac{4}{5} - \dfrac{3}{5}$

23. $\dfrac{2}{3} - \dfrac{1}{3}$ ◯ $\dfrac{7}{12} - \dfrac{5}{12}$

24. $\dfrac{3}{8} - \dfrac{3}{8}$ ◯ $\dfrac{9}{16} - \dfrac{5}{16}$

25. $\dfrac{5}{5} - \dfrac{3}{5}$ ◯ $\dfrac{10}{10} - \dfrac{7}{10}$

26. $\dfrac{7}{8} - \dfrac{5}{8}$ ◯ $\dfrac{13}{16} - \dfrac{11}{16}$

Homework Practice

Subtract Like Fractions

Subtract. Write each difference in simplest form.

1. $\frac{8}{5} - \frac{2}{5} =$ _____

2. $\frac{5}{9} - \frac{1}{9} =$ _____

3. $\frac{6}{8} - \frac{5}{8} =$ _____

4. $\frac{3}{4} - \frac{2}{4} =$ _____

5. $\frac{9}{9} - \frac{3}{9} =$ _____

6. $\frac{7}{8} - \frac{2}{8} =$ _____

7. $\frac{2}{2} - \frac{1}{2} =$ _____

8. $\frac{4}{5} - \frac{3}{5} =$ _____

9. $\frac{12}{15} - \frac{3}{15} =$ _____

10. $\frac{6}{7} - \frac{1}{7} =$ _____

Spiral Review

Add. Write each sum in simplest form. (Lesson 10–1)

11. $\frac{1}{9} + \frac{5}{9} =$ _____

12. $\frac{4}{6} + \frac{1}{6} =$ _____

13. $\frac{2}{3} + \frac{1}{3} =$ _____

14. $\frac{7}{8} + \frac{2}{8} =$ _____

15. $\frac{2}{10} + \frac{1}{10} =$ _____

16. $\frac{1}{3} + \frac{6}{3} =$ _____

17. $\frac{5}{8} + \frac{3}{8} =$ _____

18. $\frac{5}{15} + \frac{5}{15} =$ _____

19. $\frac{7}{8} + \frac{1}{8} =$ _____

20. $\frac{2}{8} + \frac{5}{8} =$ _____

21. $\frac{5}{8} + \frac{11}{8} =$ _____

22. $\frac{6}{7} + \frac{2}{7} =$ _____

10-2

Problem-Solving Practice

Subtract Like Fractions

Solve. Write your answer in simplest form.

1. Beth bought $\frac{5}{6}$ pound of provolone cheese and $\frac{3}{6}$ pound of mozzarella cheese. How much more provolone than mozzarella did she buy?

_____

2. An aquarium was $\frac{9}{10}$ full with water. After cleaning the aquarium, it was $\frac{4}{10}$ full with water. What fraction of the water was drained while cleaning the aquarium?

_____

3. On a class trip to the museum, $\frac{5}{8}$ of the students saw the dinosaurs and $\frac{2}{8}$ of the students saw the jewelry collection. What fraction of students saw the dinosaurs over the jewelry collection?

_____

4. At a family reunion, $\frac{7}{12}$ of Vanessa's family brought a dinner item and $\frac{5}{12}$ brought a dessert item. What part of her family brought dinner over dessert?

_____

5. Julio read $\frac{5}{9}$ of a book the first week and $\frac{2}{9}$ of the same book the second week. How much of the book did he have left to read?

_____

6. Brad completed $\frac{3}{10}$ of his homework immediately after school and $\frac{5}{10}$ of his homework after dinner. How much of his homework does he have left to do?

_____

Name _____ Date _____

Enrich

Fraction Puzzles

In the puzzles below, the sum of the fractions in each row is the same as the sum of the fractions in each column. Use your knowledge of adding and subtracting fractions to find the missing fractions. *Hint*: **Remember to check the fractions for like denominators before adding.**

Puzzle 1

$\frac{3}{20}$	$\frac{9}{20}$		
	$\frac{2}{20}$		$\frac{2}{20}$
$\frac{2}{20}$	$\frac{4}{20}$		$\frac{7}{20}$
	$\frac{3}{20}$	$\frac{6}{20}$	

Puzzle 2

$\frac{9}{15}$		$\frac{3}{15}$	$\frac{2}{15}$
$\frac{4}{15}$		$\frac{0}{15}$	
$\frac{2}{15}$		$\frac{7}{15}$	
$\frac{1}{15}$	$\frac{2}{15}$		$\frac{7}{15}$

Puzzle 3

$\frac{6}{25}$	$\frac{3}{25}$	$\frac{11}{25}$	
			$\frac{2}{25}$
$\frac{2}{25}$			$\frac{6}{25}$
$\frac{3}{25}$	$\frac{4}{25}$	$\frac{1}{25}$	$\frac{12}{25}$

Puzzle 4

$\frac{8}{16}$	$\frac{1}{16}$		$\frac{2}{16}$
	$\frac{7}{16}$		$\frac{2}{16}$
$\frac{3}{16}$			$\frac{2}{16}$
$\frac{0}{16}$	$\frac{2}{16}$	$\frac{4}{16}$	$\frac{6}{16}$

CHALLENGE Create your own fraction puzzle using a box of 5 rows and 5 columns.

Name _____ Date _____

Reteach

Add Unlike Fractions

When adding fractions with unlike denominators, it helps to write the problems in vertical form.

Add $\frac{7}{8} + \frac{2}{3}$.

Step 1

Find the least common denominator (LCD).

Multiples of 3:
3, 6, 9, 12, 15, 18, 21, **24**, . . .

Multiples of 8: 8, 16, **24**, . . .

The LCD is 24.

Step 2

Rename each fraction using the LCD.

$$\frac{7}{8} = \frac{21}{24}$$
$$\frac{2}{3} = \frac{16}{24}$$

Step 3

Write the problems in vertical form.

Add.

$$\frac{7}{8} = \frac{21}{24}$$
$$+\frac{2}{3} = +\frac{16}{24}$$
$$\frac{37}{24} = 1\frac{13}{24}$$

Add. Write your answer in simplest form.

1. $\frac{3}{8} + \frac{5}{6}$

Multiples of 8: _____

Multiples of 6: _____

LCD: _____

So, $\frac{3}{8} + \frac{5}{6} =$ _____

2. $\frac{11}{12} + \frac{3}{4}$

Multiples of 12: _____

Multiples of 4: _____

LCD: _____

So, $\frac{11}{12} + \frac{3}{4} =$ _____

3. $\frac{4}{5} + \frac{2}{3} =$ _____

4. $\frac{3}{5} + \frac{9}{10} =$ _____

5. $\frac{9}{10} + \frac{5}{6} =$ _____

6. $\frac{7}{10} + \frac{3}{4} =$ _____

7. $\frac{5}{8} + \frac{2}{5} =$ _____

8. $\frac{3}{4} + \frac{5}{6} =$ _____

9. $\frac{1}{2} + \frac{3}{8} =$ _____

10. $\frac{1}{4} + \frac{3}{8} =$ _____

11. $\frac{3}{5} + \frac{3}{4} =$ _____

12. $\frac{7}{12} + \frac{1}{3} =$ _____

13. $\frac{5}{6} + \frac{5}{8} =$ _____

14. $\frac{7}{10} + \frac{2}{5} =$ _____

Name _____ Date _____

Skills Practice

Add Unlike Fractions

Add. Write your answer in simplest form.

1. $\dfrac{1}{2}$
$+\dfrac{1}{5}$

2. $\dfrac{2}{5}$
$+\dfrac{7}{10}$

3. $\dfrac{5}{8}$
$+\dfrac{3}{16}$

4. $\dfrac{3}{5}$
$+\dfrac{3}{20}$

5. $\dfrac{9}{10}$
$+\dfrac{7}{10}$

6. $\dfrac{7}{12}$
$+\dfrac{1}{3}$

7. $\dfrac{9}{10}$
$+\dfrac{2}{5}$

8. $\dfrac{3}{16}$
$+\dfrac{3}{8}$

9. $\dfrac{3}{4}$
$+\dfrac{2}{5}$

10. $\dfrac{7}{12}$
$+\dfrac{3}{4}$

11. $\dfrac{2}{3}$
$+\dfrac{3}{8}$

12. $\dfrac{9}{20}$
$+\dfrac{3}{5}$

13. $\dfrac{7}{16} + \dfrac{3}{8} =$ _____

14. $\dfrac{5}{6} + \dfrac{7}{12} =$ _____

15. $\dfrac{15}{16} + \dfrac{5}{8} =$ _____

16. $\dfrac{17}{20} + \dfrac{3}{4} =$ _____

17. $\dfrac{1}{4} + \dfrac{4}{5} =$ _____

18. $\dfrac{1}{2} + \dfrac{1}{5} =$ _____

19. $\dfrac{5}{8} + \dfrac{2}{5} =$ _____

20. $\dfrac{7}{10} + \dfrac{1}{2} =$ _____

21. $\dfrac{5}{6} + \dfrac{5}{8} =$ _____

22. $\dfrac{5}{8} + \dfrac{3}{10} =$ _____

23. $\dfrac{3}{5} + \dfrac{1}{4} =$ _____

24. $\dfrac{5}{6} + \dfrac{7}{9} =$ _____

25. $\dfrac{9}{10} + \dfrac{7}{20} =$ _____

26. $\dfrac{3}{5} + \dfrac{5}{6} =$ _____

27. $\dfrac{5}{8} + \dfrac{35}{12} =$ _____

Problem Solving
Solve.

28. After school, Michael walks $\dfrac{3}{5}$ mile to the park and then walks $\dfrac{3}{4}$ mile to his house. How far does Michael walk from school to his house?

29. When Rachel walks to school on the sidewalk, she walks $\dfrac{7}{10}$ mile. When she takes the shortcut across the field, she walks $\dfrac{1}{4}$ mile less. How long is the shorter route?

_____   _____

Name _____ Date _____

Homework Practice

Add Unlike Fractions

Add. Write your answer in simplest form.

1. $\frac{2}{3}$ $+\frac{3}{5}$

2. $\frac{2}{3}$ $+\frac{5}{9}$

3. $\frac{3}{4}$ $+\frac{5}{8}$

4. $\frac{2}{7}$ $+\frac{5}{14}$

5. $\frac{1}{2}$ $+\frac{5}{6}$

6. $\frac{11}{12}$ $+\frac{3}{4}$

7. $\frac{5}{12}$ $+\frac{1}{4}$

8. $\frac{7}{15}$ $+\frac{1}{6}$

9. $\frac{8}{9}$ $+\frac{2}{3}$

10. $\frac{5}{6}$ $+\frac{3}{8}$

11. $\frac{7}{15}$ $+\frac{1}{3}$

12. $\frac{3}{4}$ $+\frac{3}{10}$

13. $\frac{2}{9}$ $+\frac{5}{6}$

14. $\frac{4}{5}$ $+\frac{3}{4}$

15. $\frac{11}{12}$ $+\frac{7}{8}$

16. $\frac{7}{10}$ $+\frac{1}{6}$

17. $\frac{7}{8}$ $+\frac{2}{3}$

18. $\frac{9}{10}$ $+\frac{9}{15}$

19. $\frac{2}{5} + \frac{7}{10} =$ _____

20. $\frac{5}{6} + \frac{4}{9} =$ _____

21. $\frac{2}{3} + \frac{1}{4} =$ _____

22. $\frac{7}{10} + \frac{1}{5} =$ _____

23. $\frac{3}{4} + \frac{1}{3} =$ _____

24. $\frac{5}{6} + \frac{2}{9} =$ _____

25. $\frac{2}{5} + \frac{3}{10} =$ _____

26. $\frac{3}{4} + \frac{2}{3} =$ _____

27. $\frac{3}{10} + \frac{3}{4} =$ _____

Spiral Review

Solve.

28. Cathy spent $\frac{2}{5}$ of an hour on her French assignment and $\frac{4}{5}$ of an hour on her English report. How much more time did she spend on her English report than her French assignment? Write your answer in simplest form.

29. On saturday, Jason spent $\frac{9}{10}$ of his time skateboarding and $\frac{1}{10}$ of his time reading. How much more time did Jason spend skateboarding than reading?

_____

_____

Name _____ Date _____

Problem-Solving Practice

Add Unlike Fractions

Solve. Write your answer in simplest form.

1. Elizabeth made an English muffin pizza using $\frac{1}{4}$ cup of cheese and $\frac{1}{10}$ cup of sausage. How many cups of toppings did she use?

   _____

2. Eric delivers $\frac{1}{5}$ of the newspapers in the neighborhood, and Anita delivers $\frac{1}{2}$ of them. Eric and Anita deliver what fraction of the papers?

   _____

Solve. Write your answer in simplest form.

3. Christie took a social studies test on Monday. Two-fifths of the questions were multiple-choice, and $\frac{3}{7}$ of the question were true-false questions. What part of the total number of questions are either multiple choice or true-false questions?

   _____

4. Brian was hungry and wanted to eat $\frac{3}{8}$ of a pie. His friend was even hungrier and wanted to eat $\frac{3}{4}$ of a pie. Will one pie be enough for the two boys? If not, how much of another pie is needed?

   _____

Solve. Write your answer in simplest form.

5. Sue took a survey in the fifth grade and found that $\frac{1}{4}$ of the students wore sandals, $\frac{4}{7}$ wore tennis shoes, and $\frac{1}{8}$ wore loafers. What part of the students wore one of these three types of shoes?

   _____

6. Long's car is being repaired. His brother takes him where he needs to go from 9:00 A.M. to noon. His sister takes him where he needs to go from 2:00 P.M. to 7:00 P.M. Change these time periods to fractions of a day. In simplest terms, what part of the day does he have transportation to take him where he needs to go?

   _____

10-3

Enrich

Add Unlike Fractions

The fractions in the squares are addends. Write the pair of addends that will give each sum.

| $\dfrac{2}{3}$ | $\dfrac{3}{5}$ | $\dfrac{3}{8}$ | $\dfrac{1}{12}$ |

| $\dfrac{3}{4}$ | $\dfrac{7}{10}$ | $\dfrac{2}{5}$ | $\dfrac{5}{6}$ |

| $\dfrac{1}{16}$ | $\dfrac{7}{8}$ |

1. _____ + _____ = $1\dfrac{3}{10}$

2. _____ + _____ = $1\dfrac{11}{40}$

3. _____ + _____ = $1\dfrac{5}{12}$

4. _____ + _____ = $\dfrac{15}{16}$

5. _____ + _____ = $1\dfrac{7}{20}$

6. _____ + _____ = $\dfrac{23}{24}$

7. _____ + _____ = $1\dfrac{1}{15}$

8. _____ + _____ = $\dfrac{7}{16}$

9. _____ + _____ = $\dfrac{11}{12}$

10. _____ + _____ = $1\dfrac{11}{30}$

Name _____ Date _____

Reteach

Subtract Unlike Fractions

You can draw models to help subtract fractions with unlike denominators.

Subtract $\frac{3}{4} - \frac{1}{3}$.

Show models for $\frac{3}{4}$ and $\frac{1}{3}$.

| $\frac{1}{4}$ | $\frac{1}{4}$ | $\frac{1}{4}$ | $\frac{3}{4}$ | $\frac{1}{3}$ | $\frac{1}{3}$ |

Find the LCD of $\frac{3}{4}$ and $\frac{1}{3}$.

Multiples of 4: 4, 8, **12,** ...

Multiples of 3: 3, 6, 9, **12,** ...

The LCD of $\frac{3}{4}$ and $\frac{1}{3}$ is 12

Use models to show how many twelfths are in $\frac{3}{4}$, and how many twelfths are in $\frac{1}{3}$.

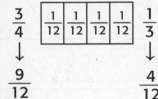

$$\frac{3}{4} \downarrow \frac{9}{12} \qquad \frac{1}{3} \downarrow \frac{4}{12}$$

Take away models to subtract $\frac{4}{12}$.

$$\frac{3}{4} - \frac{1}{3} \downarrow \quad \downarrow \quad \frac{9}{12} - \frac{4}{12} = \frac{5}{12}$$

So, $\frac{3}{4} - \frac{1}{3} = \frac{5}{12}$.

Use the fraction models to subtract the fractions.
Write your answer in simplest form.

1.

| $\frac{1}{4}$ | $\frac{1}{4}$ | $\frac{1}{4}$ |

$$\frac{3}{4} - \frac{5}{12}$$

$$\frac{\boxed{}}{12} - \frac{\boxed{}}{12} = \underline{}$$

2.

| $\frac{1}{2}$ |

$$\frac{1}{2} - \frac{2}{5}$$

$$\frac{\boxed{}}{\boxed{}} - \frac{\boxed{}}{\boxed{}} = \underline{}$$

3.

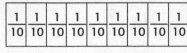

$$\frac{9}{10} - \frac{3}{5}$$

$$\frac{\boxed{}}{\boxed{}} - \frac{\boxed{}}{\boxed{}} = \underline{}$$

Subtract. You may use models. Write your answer in simplest form.

4. $\frac{1}{2} - \frac{3}{8} =$ _____

5. $\frac{5}{6} - \frac{7}{12} =$ _____

6. $\frac{11}{12} - \frac{1}{4} =$ _____

7. $\frac{2}{3} - \frac{1}{2} =$ _____

8. $\frac{9}{20} - \frac{2}{5} =$ _____

9. $\frac{7}{8} - \frac{1}{3} =$ _____

Name _____ Date _____

Skills Practice

Subtract Unlike Fractions

Write the subtraction sentence shown by each model.
Write the difference in simplest form.

1.

$\frac{1}{5}$	$\frac{1}{5}$	$\frac{1}{5}$

$\frac{1}{10}$	$\frac{1}{10}$	$\frac{1}{10}$	$\frac{1}{10}$	$\frac{1}{10}$	$\cdot\frac{1}{10}$

_____

2.

$\frac{1}{3}$	$\frac{1}{3}$

$\frac{1}{6}$	$\frac{1}{6}$	$\frac{1}{6}$	$\frac{1}{6}$

_____

3.

$\frac{1}{4}$	$\frac{1}{4}$	$\frac{1}{4}$

$\frac{1}{12}$	$\frac{1}{12}$	$\frac{1}{12}$	$\frac{1}{12}$	$\frac{1}{12}$	$\frac{1}{12}$	$\frac{1}{12}$	$\frac{1}{12}$	$\frac{1}{12}$

_____

4.

$\frac{1}{4}$

$\frac{1}{10}$	$\frac{1}{10}$	$\frac{1}{10}$	$\frac{1}{10}$	$\frac{1}{10}$	$\frac{1}{10}$

_____

5.

$\frac{1}{8}$	$\frac{1}{8}$	$\frac{1}{8}$

$\frac{1}{12}$	$\frac{1}{12}$	$\frac{1}{12}$	$\frac{1}{12}$	$\frac{1}{12}$	$\frac{1}{12}$	$\frac{1}{12}$	$\frac{1}{12}$	$\frac{1}{12}$

_____

6.

$\frac{1}{6}$	$\frac{1}{6}$	$\frac{1}{6}$	$\frac{1}{6}$	$\frac{1}{6}$	$\frac{1}{6}$

_____

Subtract. Write your answer in simplest form.

7. $\frac{7}{12} - \frac{1}{4} =$

8. $\frac{1}{2} - \frac{1}{3} =$

9. $\frac{9}{10} - \frac{2}{5} =$

10. $\frac{5}{8} - \frac{1}{4} =$

11. $\frac{11}{20} - \frac{3}{10} =$

12. $\frac{11}{12} - \frac{1}{3} =$

13. $\frac{7}{10} - \frac{1}{2} =$

14. $\frac{3}{4} - \frac{2}{3} =$

15. $\frac{5}{6} - \frac{3}{4} =$

16. $\frac{3}{4} - \frac{3}{5} =$

17. $\frac{11}{12} - \frac{1}{4} =$

18. $\frac{4}{5} - \frac{1}{2} =$

Problem Solving

Solve.

19. The distance around a lily pond is $\frac{7}{10}$ mile. Rocks have been placed for $\frac{1}{4}$ mile along the pond's edge. How much of the edge does not have rocks?

20. The first $\frac{1}{5}$ mile of a $\frac{3}{4}$ mile path through a rose garden is paved with bricks. How much of the path is not paved with bricks?

_____   _____

Name _____ Date _____

Homework Practice

Subtract Unlike Fractions

Subtract. Write your answer in simplest form.

1. $\dfrac{2}{3}$
    $-\dfrac{3}{5}$

2. $\dfrac{2}{3}$
    $-\dfrac{5}{9}$

3. $\dfrac{3}{4}$
    $-\dfrac{5}{8}$

4. $\dfrac{5}{7}$
    $-\dfrac{5}{14}$

5. $\dfrac{1}{2}$
    $-\dfrac{1}{6}$

6. $\dfrac{11}{12}$
    $-\dfrac{3}{4}$

7. $\dfrac{5}{12}$
    $-\dfrac{1}{4}$

8. $\dfrac{7}{15}$
    $-\dfrac{1}{6}$

9. $\dfrac{8}{9}$
    $-\dfrac{2}{3}$

10. $\dfrac{5}{6}$
    $-\dfrac{3}{8}$

11. $\dfrac{7}{15}$
    $-\dfrac{1}{3}$

12. $\dfrac{3}{4}$
    $-\dfrac{4}{10}$

13. $\dfrac{8}{9}$
    $-\dfrac{5}{6}$

14. $\dfrac{4}{5}$
    $-\dfrac{3}{4}$

15. $\dfrac{11}{12}$
    $-\dfrac{7}{8}$

16. $\dfrac{7}{10}$
    $-\dfrac{1}{6}$

17. $\dfrac{7}{4}$
    $-\dfrac{5}{8}$

18. $\dfrac{9}{10}$
    $-\dfrac{9}{15}$

19. $\dfrac{4}{5} - \dfrac{7}{10} = $ _____

20. $\dfrac{5}{6} - \dfrac{4}{9} = $ _____

21. $\dfrac{2}{3} - \dfrac{1}{4} = $ _____

22. $\dfrac{7}{10} - \dfrac{1}{5} = $ _____

23. $\dfrac{3}{4} - \dfrac{1}{3} = $ _____

24. $\dfrac{5}{6} - \dfrac{2}{9} = $ _____

25. $\dfrac{2}{5} - \dfrac{1}{6} = $ _____

26. $\dfrac{3}{4} - \dfrac{2}{3} = $ _____

27. $\dfrac{9}{10} - \dfrac{3}{4} = $ _____

Spiral Review

Solve.

28. Clifton spent $\dfrac{2}{3}$ hour practicing guitar. He spent $\dfrac{1}{6}$ hour changing the strings on his guitar. How much time did he spend practicing and changing the strings?

29. In the new den, $\dfrac{1}{6}$ of the walls will be made of glass blocks, and $\dfrac{1}{8}$ will be covered with tile. What fraction of the room will be covered with glass blocks and tile?

_____

_____

10-4

Problem-Solving Practice

Subtract Unlike Fractions

Solve. Write your answer in simplest form.

1. Steve watched television for $\frac{3}{4}$ hour on Monday and $\frac{5}{6}$ hour on Tuesday. How many more hours did he watch television on Tuesday?

   _____

2. Deanna uses $\frac{2}{3}$ cup flour and $\frac{1}{4}$ cup shortening in a recipe. How much more flour than shortening does she use?

   _____

Solve. Write your answer in simplest form.

3. Marsha and her friend, Tina, are making table decorations for a party. Marsha made $\frac{2}{9}$ of a decoration in half an hour. Tina can make $\frac{2}{3}$ of a decoration in the same amount of time. How much more of a decoration can Tina make in half an hour?

   _____

4. Kyle planted flowers in the front of the school. He planted $\frac{11}{16}$ of the plants on Friday and $\frac{1}{4}$ of the plants on Saturday. On which day did he plant more flowers? What is the difference in the amount of flowers he planted on the two days?

   _____

Solve. Write your answer in simplest form.

5. Shawn rides his bicycle $\frac{9}{10}$ mile to school. On his way to school, he stops at Mike's house, which is $\frac{1}{5}$ mile from Shawn's house. Then they both ride to Jose's house, which is $\frac{2}{7}$ mile from Mike's house. How far is it from Jose's house to the school?

6. After school, Laura babysits one child for 50 minutes. They rest for 10 minutes, read for 15 minutes, and play for the rest of the time. Write the total babysitting time, the resting time, and the reading time, as fractions of an hour.

   _____

   Use these fractions to find the fraction of an hour they play.

   _____

10-4

Enrich

Subtract Unlike Fractions

Play "Five-in-a-Row" with a partner. You will need a coin.

- Player 1 selects any two fractions on the game board.
  Then the player tosses the coin. If the coin lands heads up, the player finds the sum of the fractions. If the coin lands tails up, the player finds the difference.

- Player 2 checks Player 1's sum or difference.
  If it is correct, Player 1 writes an X in each box containing the fractions added or subtracted

- Player 2 takes a turn and writes an O in each box.

- The player who marks five Xs or five Os in row wins.
  If no more boxes can be marked, the player who marked more boxes is the winner.

$\frac{1}{10}$	$\frac{3}{5}$	$\frac{7}{8}$	$\frac{1}{4}$	$\frac{4}{5}$
$\frac{3}{4}$	$\frac{1}{2}$	$\frac{5}{12}$	$\frac{1}{8}$	$\frac{7}{20}$
$\frac{5}{6}$	$\frac{3}{8}$	$\frac{1}{6}$	$\frac{3}{10}$	$\frac{1}{5}$
$\frac{1}{12}$	$\frac{2}{3}$	$\frac{2}{5}$	$\frac{5}{6}$	$\frac{1}{2}$
$\frac{5}{8}$	$\frac{1}{4}$	$\frac{7}{10}$	$\frac{3}{8}$	$\frac{1}{3}$

Chapter Resources

Name _____ Date _____

Reteach

Problem-Solving Strategy: Determine Reasonable Answers

Linden buys $1\frac{3}{4}$ pounds of cashew nuts and $1\frac{1}{4}$ pounds of peanuts. He mixes the nuts together. About how many pounds of nuts are there altogether?

Step 1 Understand	**What do you know?** • You know the amount of cashew nuts and the amount of peanuts. **What do you need to find?** You need to find about how many pounds of nuts there are altogether.
Step 2 Plan	You can use estimation to find a reasonable answer.
Step 3 Solve	Round each amount to the nearest whole number. Then add. $1\frac{3}{4} \rightarrow 2 \qquad 1\frac{1}{4} \rightarrow 1$ Linden bought about 2 + 1 or 3 pounds of nuts.
Step 4 Check	**Is the answer reasonable?** Yes, because $1\frac{3}{4} + 1\frac{1}{4} = 3$.

10-5

Reteach

Problem-Solving Strategy: Determine Reasonable Answers

Solve. Determine which answer is reasonable.

1. Renata bought 0.85 pound of pine nuts and 0.9 pound of macadamia nuts. Is 1.5 pounds, 2 pounds, or 2.5 pounds a more reasonable estimate for how many pounds of nuts she purchased altogether?

   _____

2. One container has $2\frac{5}{8}$ pounds of pineapple and another has $1\frac{7}{8}$ pounds of pineapple. Sam buys both containers. Which is a more reasonable estimate for how many pounds of pineapple he bought in all: 4 pounds, 5 pounds, or 6 pounds?

   _____

3. From the beginning of a trail, Claire hiked $4\frac{3}{8}$ miles to the lake. Then she hiked $2\frac{5}{8}$ miles to the nature center. Is 5 miles, 6 miles, or 7 miles a more reasonable estimate for how far Claire hiked altogether?

   _____

4. At the beginning of the week there were 2.85 pounds of jelly beans in a jar. By the end of the week, there were 1.7 pounds of jelly beans in the jar. Which is a more reasonable estimate for how many jelly beans were eaten during the week: 1 pound, 2 pounds, or 2.5 pounds?

   _____

5. In the morning, Kevin feeds his cat $\frac{1}{2}$ of a can of cat food, in the afternoon, the cat eats $\frac{1}{4}$ of a can of food, and in the evening, the cat eats $\frac{3}{4}$ of a can of food. Which is a more reasonable estimate for the amount of food the cat eats throughout the day: 1 can, 2 cans, or 3 cans?

   _____

6. A DVD player costs $154.98. A portable digital music player costs $174.49. Is $15, $20, or $25 a more reasonable estimate for how much more the digital music player costs?

   _____

Name _____ Date _____

Skills Practice

Problem-Solving Strategy: Determine Reasonable Answers

Solve. Determine which answer is reasonable.

1. Ms. Montoya makes $2\frac{3}{4}$ pounds of goat cheese in the morning. In the afternoon, she makes $1\frac{1}{4}$ pounds of goat cheese. Is 3 pounds, 4 pounds, or 5 pounds a more reasonable estimate for how much goat cheese Ms. Montoya makes in one day?

_____

2. The Wilsons decide to churn butter for a family project. The boys in the family make 2.5 pounds of butter. The girls in the family make 4.7 pounds of butter. Which is a more reasonable estimate for how much more butter the girls made than the boys: 2 pounds, 3 pounds, or 4 pounds?

_____

3. Clara picks 5.75 bushels of apples. Franz picks 3.25 bushels of apples. Is 2 bushels, 3 bushels, or 4 bushels a more reasonable estimate for how many more bushels Clara picked than Franz?

_____

4. On Monday, Tina makes 4.7 pounds of raisins from grapes. On Tuesday, she makes 3.8 pounds of raisins. Which is a more reasonable estimate for about how many pounds of raisins she made in all: 7 pounds, 8 pounds, or 9 pounds?

_____

5. Miguel picked 3.68 pounds of grapes last week. This week, he picks 2.27 pounds of grapes. Is 5 pounds, 6 pounds, or 7 pounds a more reasonable estimate for how many pounds Miguel picked altogether?

_____

Name _____ Date _____

Homework Practice

Problem-Solving Strategy: Determine Reasonable Answers

Solve. Determine which answer is reasonable.

1. Marci found $1.42 in her coat pocket. She had $4.85 in her backpack. Is $5.50, $6.50, or $7.50 a more reasonable estimate for how much money she had altogether?

2. James and a friend picked strawberries. James picked $4\frac{3}{5}$ pounds, and his friend picked $5\frac{4}{5}$ pounds. Which is a more reasonable estimate for how many pounds they picked altogether: 10 pounds, 11 pounds, or 12 pounds?

_____

_____

3. After school, Philipe spent $1\frac{3}{4}$ hour at baseball practice, $2\frac{1}{4}$ hour on homework, and $\frac{1}{4}$ hour getting ready for bed. Which is a more reasonable estimate for how long he spent on his activities: 3 hours, 4 hours, or 5 hours?

4. Lynn went shopping at a local store. She bought 5 CDs, for $15.99 each, some candy for $1.79, and gloves for $5.89. Is $85, $88, or $90 a more reasonable estimate for how much money she spent altogether?

_____

_____

Spiral Review

Subtract. Write each difference in simplest form. (Lesson 10–4)

5. $\frac{3}{6} - \frac{2}{12} =$ _____

6. $\frac{5}{5} - \frac{9}{15} =$ _____

7. $\frac{1}{2} - \frac{2}{8} =$ _____

8. $\frac{3}{4} - \frac{3}{8} =$ _____

9. $\frac{10}{12} - \frac{1}{2} =$ _____

10. $\frac{8}{9} - \frac{2}{3} =$ _____

11. $\frac{4}{5} - \frac{12}{20} =$ _____

12. $\frac{2}{3} - \frac{7}{15} =$ _____

Name _____ Date _____

Enrich

Dr. Ken's Computer Cures

Use the data from the advertisement to solve the problems.
Explain your answers.

```
┌─────────────────────────────────────────────┐
│         —Dr. Ken's Computer Cures—            │
│                                               │
│   Repairs at Ken's: $49 per hour              │
│   House calls: $75 flat fee, plus $79 per hour│
│   Web Site Design: $55 per hour               │
│   Computer Tutoring: $40 per hour             │
│   Network Design and Setup: $65 per hour      │
│   Home Computer Setup: $200                   │
└─────────────────────────────────────────────┘
```

1. On Monday, Dr. Ken's schedule lists 3 home computer setups and 4 hours of Web site design. Dr. Ken estimates that he will earn $1,000. Is his estimate reasonable?

_____

_____

2. Dr. Ken makes a house call to Leah. He spends 3 hours fixing her computer. Leah estimates that her bill will be about $315. Is her estimate reasonable?

_____

_____

3. The Computer Whiz charges $46 per hour for Web site design. The Computer Whiz spends 22 hours designing a Web site for Regina. Regina estimates that she saved $400 by using The Computer Whiz instead of Dr. Ken. Is Regina's estimate reasonable?

_____

_____

4. Dr. Ken tutors a group of 3 people for 4 hours. He charges a group rate of $32.50 per person per hour. Dr. Ken estimates that he earns $200 more than he would have if he had tutored just one person for the same amount of time at his regular rate. Is his estimate reasonable?

_____

_____

32

Name _____ Date _____

Reteach

Estimate Sums and Differences

You can round mixed numbers to the nearest whole number to estimate sums and differences of mixed numbers. Use number lines to help you.

Estimate $5\frac{5}{8} - 2\frac{1}{5}$

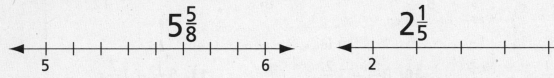

$5\frac{5}{8}$ is closer to 6 than to 5. $2\frac{1}{5}$ is closer to 2 than to 3.

$5\frac{5}{8} - 2\frac{1}{5}$
↓   ↓

$6 - 2 = 4$ So, $5\frac{5}{8} - 2\frac{1}{5}$ is about 4.

Show each mixed number on a number line and round it to the nearest whole number. Then estimate the sum or difference.

1. $3\frac{2}{5} + 4\frac{9}{10}$

$3\frac{2}{5}$ is closer to _____ than to _____. $4\frac{9}{10}$ is closer to _____ than to _____.

$3\frac{2}{5}$ + $4\frac{9}{10}$
↓   ↓

_____ + _____ = _____

Estimate by rounding each mixed number to the nearest whole number.

2. $8\frac{9}{16} - 4\frac{1}{6}$ **3.** $7\frac{9}{10} + 6\frac{7}{10}$ **4.** $9\frac{7}{12} - 1\frac{3}{8}$
   ↓   ↓   ↓   ↓   ↓   ↓

____ − ____ = ____   ____ + ____ = ____   ____ − ____ = ____

10-6

Skills Practice

Estimate Sums and Differences

Round each mixed number to the nearest whole number.

1. $7\frac{3}{4}$ _____

2. $4\frac{1}{6}$ _____

3. $8\frac{4}{10}$ _____

4. $3\frac{4}{5}$ _____

5. $2\frac{9}{16}$ _____

6. $9\frac{4}{5}$ _____

7. $1\frac{7}{8}$ _____

8. $5\frac{5}{12}$ _____

Estimate.

9. $3\frac{7}{8} + 2\frac{1}{6}$

10. $8\frac{5}{6} - 3\frac{2}{3}$

11. $5\frac{1}{8} - 1\frac{7}{8}$

12. $9\frac{7}{10} + 3\frac{4}{5}$

13. $6\frac{1}{4} + 7\frac{3}{8}$

14. $14\frac{1}{5} - 9\frac{3}{5}$

15. $18\frac{5}{16} - 9\frac{13}{16}$

16. $6\frac{11}{12} + 4\frac{5}{12}$

17. $7\frac{1}{3} + 7\frac{7}{12}$

18. $15\frac{3}{8} - 7\frac{7}{16}$

19. $9\frac{4}{5} + 6\frac{2}{3}$

20. $6\frac{11}{12} - 6\frac{1}{5}$

21. $8\frac{2}{5} + 8\frac{11}{16}$

22. $17\frac{7}{10} - 9\frac{1}{3}$

23. $7\frac{1}{3} + 9\frac{3}{8}$

24. $30\frac{7}{12} + 30\frac{1}{12}$

25. $58\frac{4}{5} - 29\frac{7}{8}$

26. $50\frac{5}{16} - 30\frac{1}{3}$

Solve.

27. Beth walks $10\frac{7}{8}$ miles in one week. She walks $2\frac{1}{4}$ fewer miles the following week. About how many miles does she walk the second week?

_____

28. Jon wants to walk at least 8 miles by the end of the week. He walks $5\frac{3}{4}$ miles by Thursday. If he walks another $2\frac{5}{8}$ miles on Friday, will he meet his goal? Explain.

_____

Name _____ Date _____

Homework Practice

Estimate Sums and Differences

Estimate.

1. $4\frac{1}{3} + \frac{8}{9}$ _____

2. $7\frac{1}{6} + \frac{8}{15}$ _____

3. $\frac{9}{10} + 3\frac{2}{3}$ _____

4. $8\frac{7}{8} - 1\frac{6}{9}$ _____

5. $1\frac{2}{10} + 3\frac{1}{9}$ _____

6. $7\frac{1}{3} + 7\frac{1}{8}$ _____

7. $3\frac{5}{8} + 6\frac{3}{5}$ _____

8. $\frac{8}{15} + 2\frac{5}{9}$ _____

9. $6\frac{7}{8} - \frac{4}{7}$ _____

10. $10\frac{7}{8} - \frac{5}{9}$ _____

Spiral Review

Solve. Determine which answer is reasonable. (Lesson 10–5)

11. A store sells 12 pounds of apples. Of those, $5\frac{1}{2}$ pounds are green apples and $2\frac{1}{4}$ are golden. Which is a more reasonable estimate for how many more pounds of green apples than golden apples were sold: 3 pounds, 4 pounds, or 5 pounds?

_____

12. Kelly has $92.63 in the bank. She wants a jacket for $91.00, but must keep at least $25 in the bank. Is $20, $25, or $30 a more reasonable estimate for how much more money she needs?

_____

35

10-6

Problem-Solving Practice

Estimate Sums and Differences

Solve.

1. Abdul works $1\frac{3}{4}$ hour one day and $1\frac{1}{3}$ hour the next day. Estimate the total number of hours he works on both days combined.

   about _____ hours

2. Anna is making cookies for the school bake sale. If she uses $1\frac{1}{8}$ pounds of flour per batch, what is the amount of flour she needs for four batches?

   about _____ pounds

3. Rachel sings in a chorus at a concert. The songs are $4\frac{3}{10}$ minutes, $7\frac{1}{12}$ minutes, and $10\frac{3}{4}$ minutes long. Estimate the amount of time the chorus spends singing.

   about _____ minutes

4. Kathy rides her bicycle to her aunt's house. It takes her $20\frac{2}{3}$ minutes to get there. She is tired when she leaves, and it takes her $24\frac{1}{6}$ minutes to ride home. What is the approximate difference in the two times?

   about _____ minutes

5. Carol wants to make a picture frame for an 8 × 10 inch photo. The long pieces of the frame need to be $12\frac{1}{8}$ inches long. The short pieces should be $10\frac{1}{4}$ inches long. Estimate the length of wood Carol must buy to make the frame.

   about _____ inches

   Would this length be the actual amount she should buy? Explain.

   _____

   _____

6. Justin plays football. On one play, he ran the ball $24\frac{1}{3}$ yards. The following play, he was tackled and lost $3\frac{2}{3}$ yards. The next play, he ran for $5\frac{1}{4}$ yards. Estimate how much farther the ball is down the field after the three plays.

   about _____ yards

10–6

Enrich

Estimate Sums and Differences

Round each mixed number to the nearest whole number. Then find
three paths of four parts each. The estimated sums and differences of
the mixed numbers on the paths must match the estimates at the finish
lines. Do not use a number more than once.

Start	Start	Start
$6\frac{7}{10}$ mi	$5\frac{9}{20}$ mi	$9\frac{7}{8}$ mi
$+\ 5\frac{3}{16}$ mi	$+\ 5\frac{3}{10}$ mi	$-\ 2\frac{3}{8}$ mi
$-\ 1\frac{11}{12}$ mi	$-\ 4\frac{3}{20}$ mi	$+\ 7\frac{9}{10}$ mi
$+\ 8\frac{11}{16}$ mi	$+\ 8\frac{2}{5}$ mi	$+\ 3\frac{1}{6}$ mi
About 20 mi	About 18 mi	About 14 mi
Finish	Finish	Finish

Name _____ Date _____

Reteach

Add Mixed Numbers

Add $2\frac{4}{6} + 4\frac{3}{6}$.

Step 1 Add the whole numbers.

$$2\frac{4}{6}$$
$$+\ 4\frac{3}{6}$$
$$\overline{6}$$

Step 2 Add the fractions.

$$2\frac{4}{6}$$
$$+\ 4\frac{3}{6}$$
$$\overline{6\frac{7}{6}}$$

Step 3 Simplify if possible.

$$6\frac{7}{6} = 7\frac{1}{6}$$

So, $2\frac{4}{6} + 4\frac{3}{6} = 7\frac{1}{6}$.

Add. Write each sum in simplest form.

1. $3\frac{5}{9}$
$+\ 4\frac{2}{9}$

2. $4\frac{1}{5}$
$+\ 5\frac{11}{15}$

3. $2\frac{1}{2}$
$+\ 4$

4. $8\frac{2}{5}$
$+\ 4\frac{1}{10}$

5. $7\frac{6}{8}$
$+\ 2\frac{1}{8}$

6. $2\frac{7}{10} + 3\frac{2}{10} =$ _____

7. $7\frac{2}{9} + 1\frac{4}{9} =$ _____

8. $8\frac{3}{14} + 2\frac{1}{7} =$ _____

9. $9\frac{3}{8} + 2\frac{1}{2} =$ _____

10. $1\frac{3}{4} + 4\frac{7}{8} =$ _____

11. $7\frac{4}{6} + 8\frac{5}{6} =$ _____

12. $1\frac{6}{15} + 9\frac{10}{15} =$ _____

13. $6\frac{3}{4} + 8\frac{4}{5} =$ _____

14. $3\frac{4}{6} + 5\frac{5}{6} =$ _____

15. $4\frac{4}{10} + 6\frac{7}{10} =$ _____

16. $8\frac{1}{16} + 4\frac{10}{16} =$ _____

17. $2\frac{6}{8} + 1\frac{5}{8} =$ _____

18. $8\frac{6}{9} + 1\frac{5}{9} =$ _____

19. $4\frac{12}{20} + 4\frac{15}{20} =$ _____

20. $5\frac{8}{12} + 2\frac{1}{4} =$ _____

Name _____ Date _____

Skills Practice

Add Mixed Numbers

Add. Write each sum in simplest form.

1. $5\frac{8}{12}$
$+ 3\frac{9}{12}$

2. $12\frac{7}{8}$
$+ 4\frac{2}{8}$

3. $13\frac{5}{10}$
$+ 4\frac{6}{10}$

4. $21\frac{8}{24}$
$+ 5\frac{7}{24}$

5. $8\frac{5}{10}$
$+ 6\frac{8}{10}$

6. $5\frac{9}{24}$
$+ 6\frac{22}{24}$

7. $5\frac{1}{5}$
$+ 2\frac{5}{15}$

8. $9\frac{4}{8}$
$+ 8\frac{1}{2}$

9. $4\frac{2}{12}$
$+ 11\frac{3}{6}$

10. $7\frac{9}{15}$
$+ 1\frac{1}{5}$

11. $4\frac{3}{10} + 5\frac{4}{10} = $ _____

12. $3\frac{7}{8} + 2\frac{4}{8} = $ _____

13. $5\frac{2}{12} + 3\frac{3}{12} = $ _____

14. $6\frac{3}{4} + 2\frac{2}{4} = $ _____

15. $1\frac{1}{12} + 3\frac{2}{12} = $ _____

16. $9\frac{4}{10} + 10\frac{3}{10} = $ _____

17. $7\frac{4}{12} + 5\frac{11}{12} = $ _____

18. $11\frac{7}{10} + 4 = $ _____

19. $2\frac{8}{12} + 4\frac{9}{12} = $ _____

20. $7\frac{6}{8} + 2\frac{7}{8} = $ _____

21. $4\frac{3}{6} + 3\frac{5}{6} = $ _____

22. $7\frac{4}{6} + 1\frac{5}{6} = $ _____

23. $2\frac{1}{4} + 4\frac{15}{20} = $ _____

24. $5\frac{3}{8} + 7\frac{4}{16} = $ _____

25. $14\frac{5}{16} + 8\frac{3}{8} = $ _____

26. $15\frac{6}{8} + 12\frac{10}{16} = $ _____

27. $9\frac{2}{12} + 4\frac{15}{18} = $ _____

28. $12\frac{1}{3} + 6\frac{2}{6} = $ _____

Solve.

29. A cave is $5\frac{2}{4}$ miles west of a waterfall. A group of hikers is $2\frac{1}{4}$ miles east of the waterfall. How far is the group of hikers from the cave?

_____

30. A mark on the side of a pier shows that the water is $4\frac{7}{8}$ ft deep. When the tide is high, the depth increases by $2\frac{3}{4}$ ft. What is the depth of the water when the tide is high?

_____

Name _____ Date _____

Homework Practice

Add Mixed Numbers

Add. Write each sum in simplest form.

1. $7\frac{15}{16} - 2\frac{11}{16} =$ _____

2. $11\frac{8}{10} + 4\frac{3}{10} =$ _____

3. $12\frac{1}{3} + 9\frac{1}{3} =$ _____

4. $18\frac{1}{6} + 9\frac{5}{6} =$ _____

5. $9\frac{2}{12} + 5\frac{1}{12} =$ _____

6. $16\frac{1}{3} + 7\frac{7}{10} =$ _____

7. $34\frac{11}{20} + 15\frac{1}{5} =$ _____

8. $64\frac{3}{4} + 37\frac{11}{12} =$ _____

9. $51\frac{2}{5} + 25\frac{3}{4} =$ _____

10. $46\frac{1}{4} + 27\frac{3}{4} =$ _____

11. $82\frac{4}{5} + 62\frac{2}{5} =$ _____

12. $23\frac{1}{8} + 15\frac{2}{5} =$ _____

13. $16\frac{1}{4} + 7\frac{11}{12} =$ _____

14. $35\frac{7}{8} + 21\frac{4}{16} =$ _____

15. $97\frac{3}{5} + 87\frac{12}{15} =$ _____

16.
$$6\frac{11}{12}$$
$$+ 4\frac{5}{12}$$
_____

17.
$$11\frac{2}{5}$$
$$+ 3\frac{2}{5}$$
_____

18.
$$14\frac{14}{16}$$
$$+ 5\frac{6}{8}$$
_____

19.
$$15\frac{1}{7}$$
$$+ 6\frac{1}{4}$$
_____

Spiral Review

Estimate. (Lesson 10–6)

20. $\frac{4}{6} + 1\frac{5}{6} =$ _____

21. $6\frac{9}{10} - 1\frac{2}{10} =$ _____

22. $19\frac{1}{10} + 5\frac{9}{10} =$ _____

23. $8\frac{11}{12} - 7\frac{1}{12} =$ _____

10-7

Problem-Solving Practice

Add Mixed Numbers

Add. Write each sum in simplest form.

1. Manuel walked $\frac{2}{3}$ of a mile to the park. He walked the same distance back home. How far did Manuel walk altogether?

   _____

2. Blanca's children are $6\frac{1}{6}$ years old and $5\frac{2}{6}$ years old. In simplest form, what are the combined ages of her children?

   _____

3. Cumberland Valley Coal Company mines $249\frac{2}{3}$ tons of coal on one day and $387\frac{2}{6}$ tons on another day. What is the total number of tons of coal mined on both days?

   _____

4. Bethany bought $2\frac{1}{2}$ pounds of bread, $3\frac{1}{4}$ pounds of meat, and $3\frac{2}{8}$ pounds of cheese to make sandwiches for a party. She also bought $2\frac{1}{4}$ pounds of tomatoes, $1\frac{4}{16}$ pounds of onions, and $2\frac{3}{4}$ pounds of lettuce.

   What is the total number of pounds of food that she bought?

   _____

5. Keith is making a canvas tent. He needs $12\frac{3}{4}$ yards of beige canvas for the top and $8\frac{2}{4}$ yards of green canvas for the bottom. How many yards of canvas does he need in all?

   _____

10-7

Enrich

Add Mixed Numbers

Find the sums for the problems in the squares. Shade pairs of adjacent squares that have the same answer to find a path through the maze.

Start

$4\frac{7}{8} + \frac{3}{8}$	$2\frac{1}{16} + 1\frac{1}{8}$	$3\frac{3}{9} + 3\frac{1}{3}$	$4\frac{15}{16} + \frac{13}{16}$
	$2\frac{5}{8} + 2\frac{7}{8}$	$4\frac{1}{20} + 2\frac{17}{20}$	$4\frac{14}{16} + 1\frac{7}{8}$
$2\frac{1}{16} + 3\frac{3}{16}$	$6\frac{5}{8} + 1\frac{5}{8}$	$8\frac{13}{16} + \frac{7}{16}$	$2\frac{1}{16} + 4\frac{11}{16}$
	$4\frac{7}{8} + 2\frac{7}{8}$	$1\frac{7}{8} + 7\frac{3}{8}$	$4\frac{9}{20} + 2\frac{17}{20}$
$2\frac{7}{16} + 5\frac{5}{16}$	$2\frac{5}{12} + 2\frac{5}{12}$	$3\frac{3}{8} + 1\frac{7}{8}$	$5\frac{4}{5} + 2\frac{8}{20}$
	$3\frac{5}{12} + \frac{5}{12}$	$3\frac{1}{20} + 2\frac{3}{20}$	$2\frac{18}{20} + 5\frac{3}{10}$
$2\frac{7}{20} + 1\frac{9}{20}$	$7\frac{1}{10} + 2$	$1\frac{14}{20} + 1\frac{7}{10}$	$3\frac{11}{12} + 3\frac{11}{12}$
	$1\frac{11}{12} + 1\frac{11}{12}$	$3\frac{3}{10} + 1\frac{9}{10}$	$2\frac{4}{6} + 3\frac{2}{3}$
$1\frac{4}{10} + 1\frac{1}{5}$	$3\frac{16}{20} + 2\frac{1}{5}$	$1\frac{3}{5} + 2\frac{16}{20}$	$3\frac{4}{6} + 1\frac{2}{3}$
	$\frac{9}{10} + 1\frac{7}{10}$	$6\frac{4}{16} + 7\frac{1}{4}$	$4\frac{1}{6} + 2\frac{1}{6}$
$1\frac{8}{10} + 8\frac{4}{5}$	$1\frac{13}{16} + 2\frac{13}{16}$	$2\frac{7}{10} + 1\frac{7}{10}$	$2\frac{13}{16} + 2\frac{9}{16}$
	$\frac{9}{10} + \frac{9}{10}$	$1\frac{3}{16} + 1\frac{9}{16}$	$2\frac{5}{10} + 2$
$3\frac{1}{20} + 1\frac{7}{20}$	$3\frac{7}{16} + 1\frac{3}{16}$	$1\frac{7}{12} + 1\frac{1}{12}$	$3\frac{1}{16} + 2\frac{5}{16}$
	$2\frac{1}{2} + 1\frac{1}{2}$	$1\frac{5}{6} + \frac{5}{6}$	$1\frac{5}{6} + 1\frac{5}{6}$

Finish

Name _____ Date _____

Reteach

Subtract Mixed Numbers

Step 1 Subtract the fractions. Regroup if necessary. **Step 2** Subtract the whole numbers. **Step 3** Simplify if possible.

$$6\frac{2}{4} \qquad 5\frac{6}{4}$$
$$-2\frac{3}{4} \rightarrow -2\frac{3}{4}$$
$$\frac{}{} \qquad \frac{}{\frac{3}{4}}$$

$$5\frac{6}{4}$$
$$-2\frac{3}{4}$$
$$\frac{}{3\frac{3}{4}}$$

$3\frac{3}{4}$ is in simplest form.

So, $6\frac{2}{4} - 2\frac{3}{4} = 3\frac{3}{4}$.

Subtract. Write each difference in simplest form.

1. $7\frac{6}{8}$
$-3\frac{3}{8}$

2. $2\frac{5}{16}$
$-1\frac{4}{16}$

3. $9\frac{4}{5}$
$-4\frac{3}{5}$

4. $21\frac{2}{16}$
$-11\frac{1}{16}$

5. $15\frac{11}{12}$
$-11\frac{6}{12}$

6. $12\frac{1}{4} - 4\frac{1}{8} =$ _____

7. $3\frac{2}{3} - 1\frac{1}{6} =$ _____

8. $6\frac{16}{20} - 2\frac{1}{4} =$ _____

9. $41\frac{11}{12} - 27\frac{10}{12} =$ _____

10. $70\frac{9}{10} - 45\frac{4}{5} =$ _____

11. $10\frac{3}{5} - 3\frac{2}{5} =$ _____

12. $3\frac{3}{8} - 1\frac{3}{4} =$ _____

13. $4\frac{6}{12} - 1\frac{1}{2} =$ _____

14. $6\frac{3}{4} - 2\frac{2}{8} =$ _____

15. $3\frac{3}{4} - 1\frac{8}{12} =$ _____

16. $18\frac{3}{6} - 1\frac{1}{6} =$ _____

17. $4\frac{3}{8} - 1\frac{1}{8} =$ _____

18. $3\frac{3}{6} - 2\frac{1}{2} =$ _____

19. $4\frac{2}{3} - 1\frac{1}{3} =$ _____

20. $25\frac{5}{8} - 17\frac{3}{8} =$ _____

10-8

Skills Practice

Subtract Mixed Numbers

Subtract. Write each difference in simplest form.

1. $10\frac{11}{16}$
$-\ 3\frac{14}{16}$

2. $8\frac{5}{8}$
$-\ 2\frac{3}{8}$

3. $9\frac{3}{5}$
$-\ 3\frac{2}{5}$

4. $5\frac{6}{8}$
$-\ 2\frac{1}{4}$

5. $8\frac{3}{5}$
$-\ 3\frac{2}{5}$

6. $7\frac{1}{2}$
$-\ 3\frac{3}{6}$

7. $2\frac{3}{4}$
$-\ 1\frac{1}{8}$

8. $4\frac{2}{16}$
$-\ 2\frac{1}{16}$

9. $9\frac{2}{3}$
$-\ 3\frac{1}{3}$

10. $2\frac{4}{5}$
$-\ 1\frac{4}{10}$

11. $15\frac{7}{12} - 8\frac{1}{2} =$ _____

12. $6\frac{7}{8} - 2\frac{7}{8} =$ _____

13. $27\frac{7}{12} - 13\frac{1}{12} =$ _____

14. $5\frac{8}{20} - 1\frac{1}{4} =$ _____

15. $10\frac{2}{3} - 7\frac{1}{3} =$ _____

16. $7\frac{1}{3} - 2\frac{1}{9} =$ _____

17. $8\frac{3}{5} - 1\frac{2}{5} =$ _____

18. $10\frac{9}{10} - 2\frac{1}{5} =$ _____

19. $12\frac{3}{10} - 6\frac{1}{10} =$ _____

20. $5\frac{9}{12} - 3\frac{9}{12} =$ _____

21. $15\frac{5}{8} - 7\frac{1}{8} =$ _____

22. $11\frac{6}{8} - 6\frac{5}{8} =$ _____

Solve.

23. Anna has $3\frac{1}{2}$ yd of fabric. She plans to use $2\frac{1}{4}$ yd for curtains. Does she have enough left to make 2 pillows that each use $1\frac{1}{2}$ yd of fabric? Explain.

24. Paula has 2 yd of elastic. One project needs a $\frac{3}{4}$-yd piece. Does she have enough for another project that needs $1\frac{1}{3}$ yd? Explain.

Name _____ Date _____

Homework Practice

Subtract Mixed Numbers

Subtract. Write each difference in simplest form.

1. $2\frac{3}{4} - 1\frac{5}{8} = $ _____

2. $3\frac{2}{3} - 2\frac{1}{6} = $ _____

3. $3\frac{7}{12} - 1\frac{5}{12} = $ _____

4. $7\frac{3}{4} - 3\frac{7}{12} = $ _____

5. $4\frac{7}{9} - 2\frac{4}{9} = $ _____

6. $6\frac{3}{4} - 4\frac{1}{4} = $ _____

7. $3\frac{1}{2} - 1\frac{1}{2} = $ _____

8. $4\frac{1}{2} - 2\frac{3}{8} = $ _____

9. $7\frac{1}{2} - 5\frac{4}{6} = $ _____

10. $12\frac{5}{8} - 4\frac{3}{8} = $ _____

11. $7\frac{9}{10} - \frac{4}{5} = $ _____

12. $13\frac{4}{5} - 4\frac{2}{5} = $ _____

13. $7\frac{20}{24} - 3\frac{6}{24} = $ _____

14. $12\frac{1}{2} - 4\frac{3}{10} = $ _____

15. $11\frac{3}{8} - 6\frac{1}{8} = $ _____

16. $14\frac{6}{10} - 6\frac{5}{10} = $ _____

17. $15\frac{3}{4} - 9\frac{2}{8} = $ _____

18. $17\frac{9}{10} - 8\frac{3}{10} = $ _____

Spiral Review

Add. Write each sum in simplest form. (Lesson 10–7)

19. $4\frac{3}{4} + 2\frac{3}{4} = $ _____

20. $5\frac{4}{9} + 4\frac{3}{9} = $ _____

21. $6\frac{5}{12} + 3\frac{1}{12} = $ _____

22. $8\frac{3}{7} + 5\frac{4}{7} = $ _____

Problem Solving Practice

Subtract Mixed Numbers

Subtract. Write each difference in simplest form.

1. A large table is $30\frac{7}{16}$ inches high. A small table is $16\frac{5}{16}$ inches high. How much higher is the larger table?

   _____

2. Brenda is $59\frac{3}{4}$ inches tall. Her sister is $48\frac{2}{8}$ inches tall. How much taller is Brenda than her sister?

   _____

3. Wilma pitches $4\frac{2}{3}$ innings in a baseball game. Nina pitches $1\frac{2}{6}$ innings in the same game. How many more innings does Wilma pitch than Nina?

   _____

4. Robert lives $3\frac{3}{10}$ miles from school. Al lives $4\frac{7}{10}$ miles from school. Who lives farther from school? How much farther?

   _____

5. Jayne needs $\frac{14}{16}$ of a yard of ribbon to decorate a banner. She has $\frac{5}{8}$ of a yard of ribbon. How much more ribbon does Jayne need?

   _____

6. Rick has a choice of buying $4\frac{3}{5}$ packages of pencils or $2\frac{2}{5}$ packages of pens. In simplest form, how many more packages of pencils than pens can he buy?

   _____

7. One year, Cumberland Valley Coal Company planted $14\frac{3}{6}$ dozen trees to help prevent erosion. The following year, they planted $20\frac{2}{3}$ dozen trees. How many more trees did they plant the second year?

   _____

Name _____ Date _____

Enrich

Subtract Mixed Numbers

Play this game with a partner. You will need a counter.

- Together choose a whole number from 5 through 10. Write it in the square at that bottom right of the game board. Place your counter on Start. Then move it one square in any direction. Find the sum or difference of the numbers in the starting square and the square you moved to. If fractions don't have like denominators, try using an equivalent fraction to find the sum or difference. Record it on a separate sheet of paper.

- Players alternate turns. On each turn, move one square. Add or subtract the number in that square to or from your previous sum or difference and record your answer. You cannot return to a square.

- The winner is the first player who reaches the target square with a sum or difference equal to the target number.

Start

$2\frac{1}{2}$	$1\frac{1}{6}$	$3\frac{5}{8}$	$2\frac{1}{8}$	$4\frac{1}{2}$	$1\frac{1}{3}$
$3\frac{1}{4}$	$2\frac{2}{5}$	$1\frac{2}{3}$	$1\frac{1}{4}$	$1\frac{4}{5}$	$2\frac{1}{4}$
$3\frac{2}{3}$	$1\frac{7}{8}$	$3\frac{1}{2}$	$1\frac{7}{10}$	$1\frac{1}{2}$	$2\frac{5}{6}$
$1\frac{3}{4}$	$1\frac{3}{8}$	$\frac{2}{3}$	$\frac{5}{8}$	$\frac{3}{5}$	$\frac{3}{8}$
$1\frac{1}{2}$	$2\frac{3}{10}$	$\frac{1}{4}$	$\frac{1}{5}$	$\frac{1}{2}$	$\frac{3}{4}$
$5\frac{1}{4}$	$2\frac{3}{4}$	$\frac{1}{8}$	$\frac{1}{6}$	$\frac{1}{3}$	Target Number _____

Name _____ Date _____

Reteach

Problem-Solving Investigation: Choose the Best Strategy

Look for a Pattern

Gregory is practicing the high jump. If he starts the bar at 3 feet 4 inches and raises it 0.5 inch after each jump, how high will the bar be on the sixth jump?

Step 1 Understand	**What facts do you know?**
	• Gregory starts the bar at _____
	• Gregory raises the bar _____ after each jump.
	What do you need to find?
	• You need to find how high _____

Step 2 Plan	**Make a plan.**
	Using a pattern will help you solve the problem.
	Organize the information in a chart.

Step 3 Solve	**Carry out your plan.**
	Make a chart. Look for a pattern in the chart.

Jump Number	1	2	3	4	5	6
Bar Height	3 feet 4 inches	3 feet 4.5 inches	3 feet 5 inches	3 feet 5.5 inches	3 feet 6 inches	

Look at the chart to find the pattern.

What is the pattern?

_____

Continue the pattern to predict the height for the sixth jump.

Jump 6: 3 feet 6 inches + 0.5 inch = _____

Using the pattern, you can expect that the bar will be set at _____ for the sixth jump.

10–9

Reteach

Problem-Solving Strategy (continued)

Step 4 Check	**Is the solution reasonable?**
	Look back at the problem.
	Have you answered the question? _____
	Does your answer make sense? _____
	Did you find a pattern and continue it? _____

Use any strategy to solve each problem.

1. On the first day of the crafts fair, 200 people show up. Each day after that, the number of people who attend the fair increases by 150. The craft fair runs for five days. How many people attend the fair on the last day?

_____

2. Find the next three numbers in the pattern below. Then describe the pattern.

   −5, 0, 5, 10, __, __, __

_____

3. Jamal, Diego, and Megan went shopping together and each bought a different type of clothing: a hat, a shirt, and a pair of shoes. Jamal did not buy something to put on his feet. Diego bought his item before the person bought the shoes. Either Megan or Diego bought the hat. What item did each person buy?

_____

4. A yellow, a green, and a blue marble are placed in a bag. If you take one marble out of the bag at a time, in how many different orders can all three marbles be removed from the bag? List all possibilities.

_____

5. Mrs. Reynolds is buying sandwiches for the 10 students in her class as a reward. If she bought at least one of each type of sandwich and spent a total of $34.00, how many of each sandwich did she buy?

Sandwiches	
Type	**Price**
Italian	$4.00
Roast Beef	$3.50
Veggie	$3.00

_____

Name _____ Date _____

Skills Practice

Problem-Solving Investigation: Choose the Best Strategy

Use any strategy to solve each problem.

1. Describe the pattern below. Then find the missing number.

10, 20, 30, _____, 50

_____

2. Fifty five families that own pets were asked what type of pets they own. Of the families surveyed, 24 have dogs, 14 have cats, and 5 have both dogs and cats. How many have neither a dog nor cat?

_____

3. A designer is making a tile mosaic. The first row of the mosaic has 1 red tile in the center. If the designer increases the number of red tiles in the center of each row by 4, how many red tiles will be in the center of the fifth row?

_____

4. Six students are sitting at a lunch table. Two more students arrive, and at the same time, three students leave. Then, four students leave, and two more arrive. How many students are at the table now?

_____

5. The sum of two whole numbers between 20 and 40 is 58. The difference of the two numbers is 12. What are the two numbers?

_____

6. Ramon has $3.50. He buys two pens that cost $0.75 each and a pencil that costs $0.40. How much money does Ramon have left?

_____

10-9

Homework Practice

Problem-Solving Investigation: Choose the Best Strategy

Use any strategy to solve each problem.

1. Describe the pattern below. Then, find the missing number.
   50, 500, ___, 50,000.

   _____

2. Melinda's mother is four times as old as Melinda. In 16 years, her mother will be twice her age. How old is Melinda now?

   _____

3. Ginny has a piece of fabric 20 yards long. How many cuts will she make if she cuts the fabric into sections that are 2 yards long?

   _____

Spiral Review

Solve. Write each answer in simplest form. (Lesson 10–8)

4. Mr. Hernandez bought $12\frac{3}{4}$ gallons of paint to paint his house. He used $10\frac{1}{4}$ gallons. How much paint was left?

   _____

5. The length of Dawn's yard is $8\frac{4}{5}$ feet. Find the width of her yard if it is $1\frac{3}{5}$ feet shorter than the length.

   _____

6. Find *eight and nine tenths minus three and four tenths*. Write your answer in words.

   _____

   _____

Name _____ Date _____

Enrich

Multi-step Problems

Solve.

1. The outer edge of a picture frame forms a square. The square picture frame has sides of 18 inches. The width of the frame is 1 inch. What is the area of the picture within the frame? Remember, area is found by multiplying length times width.

   _____

2. Sammy has a $42\frac{1}{2}$- inch-long board. He cuts three $6\frac{1}{2}$ inch long pieces of wood from the board. Does Sammy have enough wood left to make a 24 inch long shelf? Explain.

   _____

   _____

3. Theresa made a stack of cubes. Three of the cubes were $\frac{1}{2}$ inch on each side. Three of the cubes were $1\frac{1}{2}$ inches on each side. After Theresa removed a cube, the height of the stack was $4\frac{1}{2}$ inches. Which kind of cube did Theresa remove?

   _____

4. Mark was paid $10,000 to do some carpentry. He spent half of that money on suppplies and $1,000 to pay a helper. How much money did Mark earn for himself?

   _____

Name _____ Date _____

Reteach

Subtraction with Renaming

Sometimes you need to rename fractions in order to subtract them.

Subtract $6\frac{2}{4} - 2\frac{3}{4}$.

Step 1 Regroup $6\frac{2}{4}$ as $5\frac{6}{4}$.	**Step 2** Subtract the fractions.
$\begin{array}{r} 6\frac{2}{4} \\ -2\frac{3}{4} \\ \hline \end{array} \quad \rightarrow \quad \begin{array}{r} 5\frac{6}{4} \\ -2\frac{3}{4} \\ \hline \end{array}$	$\begin{array}{r} 5\frac{6}{4} \\ -2\frac{3}{4} \\ \hline \frac{3}{4} \end{array}$
Step 3 Subtract the whole numbers.	**Step 4** Simplify if possible.
$\begin{array}{r} 5\frac{6}{4} \\ -2\frac{3}{4} \\ \hline 3\frac{3}{4} \end{array}$	$3\frac{3}{4}$ is in simplest form.

So, $6\frac{1}{2} - 2\frac{3}{4} = 3\frac{3}{4}$.

Subtract. Write each difference in simplest form.

1. $\begin{array}{r} 7\frac{3}{8} \\ -3\frac{5}{8} \\ \hline \end{array}$ 2. $\begin{array}{r} 2\frac{3}{16} \\ -1\frac{9}{16} \\ \hline \end{array}$ 3. $\begin{array}{r} 9\frac{2}{5} \\ -4\frac{4}{5} \\ \hline \end{array}$ 4. $\begin{array}{r} 21\frac{7}{12} \\ -11\frac{5}{6} \\ \hline \end{array}$ 5. $\begin{array}{r} 15\frac{1}{4} \\ -11\frac{3}{4} \\ \hline \end{array}$

6. $12\frac{1}{4} - 4\frac{6}{8} =$ _____   7. $3\frac{1}{6} - 1\frac{4}{6} =$ _____   8. $6\frac{1}{5} - 2\frac{4}{5} =$ _____

9. $41\frac{2}{3} - 27\frac{11}{12} =$ _____   10. $70\frac{4}{10} - 45\frac{3}{5} =$ _____   11. $10\frac{4}{9} - 3\frac{7}{9} =$ _____

12. $3\frac{2}{8} - 1\frac{7}{8} =$ _____   13. $4\frac{5}{12} - 1\frac{3}{4} =$ _____   14. $6\frac{3}{5} - 2\frac{4}{5} =$ _____

15. $3\frac{10}{16} - 1\frac{7}{8} =$ _____   16. $18\frac{1}{3} - 13\frac{2}{3} =$ _____   17. $4\frac{3}{8} - 1\frac{7}{8} =$ _____

Name _____ Date _____

Skills Practice

Subtraction with Renaming

Subtract. Write each difference in simplest form.

1. $10\frac{6}{16}$
   $-\ 3\frac{11}{16}$
   _____

2. $8\frac{1}{3}$
   $-\ 2\frac{2}{3}$
   _____

3. $9\frac{2}{5}$
   $-\ 3\frac{4}{5}$
   _____

4. $5\frac{3}{16}$
   $-\ 2\frac{1}{2}$
   _____

5. $8\frac{1}{3}$
   $-\ 3\frac{4}{6}$
   _____

6. $7\frac{5}{9}$
   $-\ 3\frac{8}{9}$
   _____

7. $2\frac{1}{4}$
   $-\ 1\frac{3}{4}$
   _____

8. $4\frac{1}{4}$
   $-\ 2\frac{5}{8}$
   _____

9. $5\frac{2}{5} - 1\frac{4}{5} = $ _____

10. $10\frac{1}{3} - 7\frac{2}{3} = $ _____

11. $7\frac{1}{4} - 2\frac{3}{4} = $ _____

12. $8\frac{2}{6} - 1\frac{5}{6} = $ _____

13. $10\frac{1}{3} - 2\frac{5}{9} = $ _____

14. $12\frac{2}{7} - 6\frac{6}{7} = $ _____

15. $5\frac{7}{12} - 3\frac{5}{6} = $ _____

16. $15\frac{1}{8} - 7\frac{5}{8} = $ _____

17. $11\frac{1}{4} - 6\frac{1}{2} = $ _____

Find each missing number.

18. $6\frac{2}{5} - \square\frac{\square}{\square} = 1\frac{3}{5}$

19. $15\frac{3}{12} + \square\frac{\square}{\square} = 6\frac{8}{12}$

20. $10\frac{1}{3} - \square\frac{\square}{\square} = 3\frac{2}{3}$

21. $6\frac{5}{9} - \square\frac{\square}{\square} = 3\frac{6}{9}$

Solve.

22. Anna has $3\frac{1}{4}$ yd of fabric. She uses $2\frac{3}{4}$ yd for curtains. How much fabric is left over?

_____

_____

23. Paula has $2\frac{3}{6}$ yard of elastic. One project needs a $1\frac{4}{6}$ yard piece. Will she have enough elastic to make another project that uses the same amount? Explain.

_____

_____

Name _____ Date _____

Homework Practice

Subtraction with Renaming

Subtract. Write each difference in simplest form.

1. $7\dfrac{1}{4} - 4\dfrac{3}{4} =$ _____

2. $9\dfrac{2}{5} - 5\dfrac{3}{5} =$ _____

3. $6\dfrac{1}{3} - 2\dfrac{2}{3} =$ _____

4. $14\dfrac{1}{2} - 5\dfrac{1}{4} =$ _____

5. $10\dfrac{5}{8} - 6\dfrac{6}{8} =$ _____

6. $12\dfrac{1}{5} - 6\dfrac{8}{10} =$ _____

7. $5\dfrac{1}{2} - 4\dfrac{5}{6} =$ _____

8. $3\dfrac{1}{3} - 1\dfrac{2}{3} =$ _____

9. $8\dfrac{4}{7} - 2\dfrac{6}{7} =$ _____

10. $3\dfrac{1}{4} - 1\dfrac{5}{8} =$ _____

11. $9\dfrac{8}{12} - 3\dfrac{11}{12} =$ _____

12. $2\dfrac{1}{10} - 1\dfrac{2}{5} =$ _____

13. $15\dfrac{5}{9} - 8\dfrac{7}{9} =$ _____

14. $6\dfrac{7}{16} - 2\dfrac{6}{8} =$ _____

Spiral Review

Use any strategy to solve each problem. (Lesson 10–9)

- Make a graph.
- Determine reasonable answers.
- Act it out.
- Look for a pattern.

15. At a grocery store a bag of apples costs $1.79. A jar of jelly costs $0.25 less than a bag of apples. Find the total cost of these two items.

_____

16. A runner starts running 10 miles per week and adds $\dfrac{1}{2}$ mile each week. How far will she run in the seventh week?

_____

10-10

Problem-Solving Practice

Subtracting Mixed Numbers with Renaming

Solve.

1. When Shane and his family went on vacation, the pilot announced that it would take $4\frac{1}{4}$ hours to reach their destination. When the flight snack was served, they had been in flight $2\frac{3}{4}$ hours. How much longer was the flight after the snack was served?

   _____

2. Mark bought $5\frac{1}{4}$ pounds of yellow cheese and $3\frac{3}{4}$ of white cheese. How much more yellow cheese than white cheese did he buy?

   _____

3. Stella made $4\frac{5}{8}$ quarts of lemon tea for the weekend barbecue. Vincent made $2\frac{7}{8}$ quarts of mint tea for the barbecue. How much more tea did Stella make than Vincent?

   _____

4. Taylor's puppy weighs $9\frac{2}{10}$ pounds. Belinda's kitten weighs $3\frac{3}{5}$ pounds. How much more does Taylor's puppy weigh than Belinda's kitten?

   _____

5. Jillian has a piece of leather cord that is $12\frac{1}{5}$ inches long. She only needs $8\frac{4}{5}$ inches of cord to make a bracelet. How much leather cord will she trim?

   _____

Name _____ Date _____

10–10

Enrich

More Mixed Numbers

Find a path through the maze. Shade the spaces that connect two
equivalent numbers. (*Hint:* Rename fractions if you get stuck!)

$3\frac{2}{5}$		$4\frac{1}{4}$		$3\frac{3}{4}$		$3\frac{3}{8}$
	$3\frac{5}{9}$		$4\frac{19}{20}$		$4\frac{1}{2}$	
$2\frac{7}{5}$		$\frac{15}{4}$		$\frac{19}{4}$		$2\frac{7}{8}$
	$3\frac{3}{4}$		$4\frac{19}{25}$		$4\frac{3}{4}$	
$2\frac{3}{5}$		$3\frac{1}{4}$	$\frac{119}{25}$		$4\frac{1}{4}$	$2\frac{5}{8}$
	$\frac{12}{4}$		$6\frac{1}{3}$		$\frac{3}{4}$	$\frac{21}{8}$
$3\frac{3}{10}$		$7\frac{1}{2}$	$\frac{44}{25}$		$\frac{20}{3}$	$\frac{23}{8}$
	$6\frac{1}{2}$		$1\frac{1}{4}$		$6\frac{2}{3}$	$1\frac{9}{20}$
$\frac{18}{5}$		$\frac{13}{2}$	$\frac{5}{4}$		$\frac{15}{3}$	$\frac{29}{20}$
	$\frac{11}{2}$		$1\frac{1}{5}$		$6\frac{1}{4}$	$1\frac{5}{16}$
$3\frac{3}{5}$		$\frac{27}{5}$	$\frac{7}{4}$		$2\frac{11}{20}$	$1\frac{4}{5}$
	$2\frac{7}{10}$		$\frac{11}{2}$		$\frac{10}{53}$	$\frac{18}{5}$
$\frac{36}{5}$		$\frac{27}{10}$	$5\frac{1}{2}$		$\frac{51}{20}$	$\frac{53}{10}$
	$\frac{27}{100}$		$10\frac{1}{2}$		$5\frac{3}{10}$	$3\frac{3}{5}$
			$5\frac{1}{5}$		$2\frac{5}{11}$	$3\frac{3}{10}$

Name _____ Date _____

Individual Progress Checklist

Learning Mastery			Lesson	Lesson Goal	Comments
B	**D**	**M**			
			10-1	Add fractions with like denominators.	
			10-2	Subtract fractions with like denominators.	
			10-3	Add fractions with unlike denominators.	
			10-4	Subtract fractions with unlike denominators.	
			10-5	Solve problems by determining reasonable answers.	
			10-6	Estimate sums and differences of mixed numbers.	
			10-7	Add mixed numbers.	
			10-8	Subtract mixed numbers.	
			10-9	Choose the best strategy to solve a problem.	
			10-10	Subtract mixed numbers.	

B = Beginning; **D** = Developing; **M** = Mastered

Note to Parents

_____

_____

_____

_____

_____

Name _____ Date _____

Chapter Diagnostic Test

Write each fraction in simplest form.

1. $\frac{3}{6}$

2. $\frac{3}{12}$

3. $\frac{12}{20}$

4. $\frac{3}{18}$

5. Jamie made 5 out of 15 free throws. Write the fraction of free throws she made in simplest form.

1. _____

2. _____

3. _____

4. _____

5. _____

Write each improper fraction as a mixed number.

6. $\frac{9}{5}$

7. $\frac{4}{3}$

8. $\frac{12}{7}$

9. $\frac{25}{6}$

10. Victoria needs $\frac{6}{4}$ cups of raisins to make bread. Write the fraction as a mixed number.

6. _____

7. _____

8. _____

9. _____

10. _____

Estimate the sum or difference by rounding to the nearest whole number.

11. $12.2 - 8.1$

12. $3.4 + 4.9$

13. $5.3 + 2.3$

14. $13.8 - 6.1$

15. Jose bought a tie that cost $5.59 and a pair of socks that cost $3.99. About how much did he spend altogether? Round to the nearest dollar.

11. _____

12. _____

13. _____

14. _____

15. _____

Name _____ Date _____

Chapter Pretest

Write each sum in simplest form.

1. $\dfrac{2}{5} + \dfrac{2}{5}$

2. $\dfrac{8}{9} + \dfrac{3}{9}$

Replace ◯ **with >, <, or − to make a true sentence.**

3. $\dfrac{5}{6} - \dfrac{1}{6}$ ◯ $\dfrac{2}{3} - \dfrac{1}{3}$

Solve.

4. Frank has $41.35 in the bank. He wants to buy his mother a gift that costs $25.00 but he must keep at least $25.00 in the bank. How much more money does Frank need to save?

5. Yuli has a piece of wood that measures $4\dfrac{1}{5}$ feet. If each shelf she is making is $1\dfrac{4}{5}$ feet long, will she have enough for 3 shelves?

Estimate by rounding each mixed number to the nearest whole number.

6. $4\dfrac{4}{5} + 1\dfrac{4}{5}$

Subtract. Write each difference in simplest form.

7. $17\dfrac{11}{16} - 9\dfrac{5}{16}$

8. $34\dfrac{7}{9} - 21\dfrac{2}{9}$

9. $3\dfrac{1}{4} - 2\dfrac{2}{4}$

10. $17 - 5\dfrac{3}{4}$

1. _____

2. _____

3. _____

4. _____

5. _____

6. _____

7. _____

8. _____

9. _____

10. _____

Name _____ Date _____

Quiz 1 *(Lessons 10–1 through 10–5)*

Add. Write each sum in simplest form.

1. $\frac{4}{7} + \frac{2}{7}$

2. $\frac{1}{9} + \frac{7}{9}$

3. $\frac{1}{3} + \frac{2}{9}$

1. _____

2. _____

3. _____

Subtract. Write each difference in simplest form.

4. $\frac{4}{7} - \frac{3}{7}$

5. $\frac{12}{16} - \frac{8}{16}$

6. $\frac{3}{4} - \frac{1}{8}$

7. Find the difference between *six ninths and four ninths*. Write your answer in words.

4. _____

5. _____

6. _____

7. _____

Solve. Determine which answer is reasonable.

8. Andy has a stamp collection with 343 stamps. Of these, 296 are from Germany. Is 40, 50, or 60 a more reasonable estimate for how many stamps are from other countries?

8. _____

9. Mrs. Dean harvested $1\frac{1}{4}$ pounds of green peppers, $2\frac{1}{4}$ pounds of yellow peppers, and $5\frac{1}{4}$ pounds of red peppers from her garden. Is 8 pounds, 9 pounds, or 10 pounds a more reasonable estimate for how many pounds of peppers she harvested altogether?

9. _____

10. A marker costs $0.99. A pad of paper costs $1.25 more than the marker. Which is a more reasonable estimate for the total cost of both items: $2 or $3?

10. _____

Name _____ Date _____

Quiz 2 *(Lessons 10–6 through 10–8)*

Estimate by rounding each mixed number to the nearest whole number.

1. $4\frac{3}{5} + 1\frac{1}{5}$

2. $2\frac{1}{9} + 6\frac{7}{9}$

3. $\frac{10}{12} + \frac{11}{12}$

Add. Write each sum in simplest form.

4. $4\frac{4}{5} + 1\frac{3}{5}$

5. $2\frac{3}{7} + 3\frac{8}{14}$

6. $1\frac{7}{8} + \frac{7}{8}$

7. Eduardo's puppy weighed $8\frac{1}{4}$ pounds when it was born. In the first month, the puppy gained $3\frac{3}{4}$ pounds. How much does the puppy weigh now?

Subtract. Write each difference in simplest form.

8. $5\frac{2}{5} - 1\frac{3}{10}$

9. $12\frac{5}{6} - 7\frac{1}{6}$

10. $22\frac{5}{9} - 11\frac{4}{18}$

1. _____

2. _____

3. _____

4. _____

5. _____

6. _____

7. _____

8. _____

9. _____

10. _____

Name _____ Date _____

Quiz 3 *(Lessons 10–9 through 10–10)*

Solve.

1. At a clothing store, a pair of socks costs $3.44. A sweater vest costs $5.99 more than the socks. Find the total cost of these two items.

   1. _____

2. A high jumper sets the bar at 46 inches and raises the bar $\frac{1}{2}$ inch after each jump. How high will the bar be after the sixth jump?

   2. _____

3. Pauline has a piece of wood that measures $7\frac{1}{4}$ feet. If she wants to make a shelf that is $5\frac{3}{4}$ feet long, how much wood will she have left over?

   3. _____

4. Danielle has seven coins in her pocket that total $0.77. What are the seven coins that she has in her pocket?

   4. _____

Subtract. Write each difference in simplest form.

5. $1\frac{5}{8} - \frac{7}{8}$

   5. _____

6. $5\frac{1}{5} - 2\frac{3}{5}$

   6. _____

7. $6\frac{2}{9} - 3\frac{7}{9}$

   7. _____

8. $12\frac{3}{6} - 7\frac{2}{3}$

   8. _____

9. $20\frac{5}{9} - 11\frac{7}{9}$

   9. _____

Name _____ Date _____

Mid-Chapter Test (Lessons 10–1 through 10–6)

Add. Write each sum in simplest form.

1. $\frac{4}{6} + \frac{1}{6}$

2. $\frac{3}{9} + \frac{1}{3}$

3. $\frac{3}{4} + \frac{3}{12}$

1. _____

2. _____

3. _____

Solve.

4. At a clothing store, a hat costs $5.44. A pair of sunglasses costs $1.23 more than the hat. Find the total cost of these two items.

4. _____

5. A high jumper sets the bar at 42 inches and raises the bar $\frac{1}{2}$ inch after each jump. How high will the bar be after the fifth jump?

5. _____

6. Jane has a piece of rope that measures $2\frac{3}{4}$ feet. If she wants to make a plant hanger that uses $1\frac{2}{8}$ feet of rope, how much rope will she have left over?

6. _____

Estimate by rounding each mixed number to the nearest whole number.

7. $1\frac{7}{8} - 2\frac{1}{4}$

8. $6\frac{2}{5} - 2\frac{1}{6}$

9. $3\frac{2}{9} + 1\frac{7}{9}$

10. $10\frac{2}{6} + 4\frac{5}{6}$

7. _____

8. _____

9. _____

10. _____

Name _____ Date _____

Vocabulary Test

Match each word to its definition. Write your answers on the lines provided.

1. like fractions _____	**A.** the form of a fraction when the GCF of the numerator and the denominator is one
2. simplest form _____	**B.** a number in which the numerator is greater than the denominator
3. denominator _____	**C.** fractions that have the same denominator
4. improper fraction _____	**D.** the part of the fraction that tells how many of the equal parts are being used
5. numerator _____	**E.** the bottom number in a fraction
6. unlike fractions _____	**F.** fractions that have a different denominator

Assessment

Student Name _____ Date _____

Oral Assessment

Use construction paper to cut out the following 3 labeled shapes:

1			
$\frac{1}{2}$		$\frac{1}{2}$	
$\frac{1}{4}$	$\frac{1}{4}$	$\frac{1}{4}$	$\frac{1}{4}$

Read each question aloud to the student. Then write the student's answers on the lines below the questions.

1. How are these shapes labeled?

   _____

   _____

2. Let's line these shapes up against each other. Are all the shapes the same length?

   _____

3. Let's look at the shape labeled 1 and the shape labeled $\frac{1}{2}$ and $\frac{1}{2}$. Let's put them next to each other. What do you notice?

   _____

   _____

4. Look at the shape labeled $\frac{1}{2}$ and $\frac{1}{2}$. Think of a sentence you can tell me about what $\frac{1}{2}$ and $\frac{1}{2}$ equal.

   _____

5. Hold the shape labeled 1 next to the shape with labeled $\frac{1}{2}$ and $\frac{1}{2}$. Is your sentence correct? How do you know?

   _____

   _____

Oral Assessment *(continued)*

6. Now let's look at the shape labeled with the $\frac{1}{4}$s. How is it different from the first two shapes?

_____

_____

7. How many sections are there in this shape?

_____

8. Tell how you got your answer.

_____

9. Let's look at the shape labeled with the $\frac{1}{4}$s next to the shape labeled 1. Are these shapes the same length?

_____

10. How many $\frac{1}{4}$s are there in every shape labeled 1?

_____

11. How do you know?

_____

12. Tell a number sentence about the shape with the $\frac{1}{4}$s.

_____

13. Let's look at the shape labeled $\frac{1}{2} + \frac{1}{2}$ next to the shape labeled $\frac{1}{4} + \frac{1}{4} + \frac{1}{4} + \frac{1}{4}$. Tell how these shapes are related.

_____

_____

14. How do you know?

_____

15. Can you think of a time when you used fractions?

_____

Name _____ Date _____

Chapter Project Rubric

Score	Explanation
3	Student successfully completed the chapter project. Student demonstrated appropriate use of chapter information in completing the chapter project.
2	Student completed the chapter project with partial success. Student partially demonstrated appropriate use of chapter information in completing the chapter project.
1	Student did not complete the chapter project or completed it with little success. Student demonstrated very little appropriate use of chapter information in completing the chapter project.
0	Student did not complete the chapter project. Student demonstrated inappropriate use of chapter information in completing the chapter project.

10

Foldables® Rubric

Add and Subtract Fractions

Two-Tab Foldable

Score	Explanation
3	Student properly assembled Foldables® graphic organizer according to instructions. Student recorded information related to the chapter in the manner directed by the Foldables graphic organizer. Student used the Foldables graphic organizer as a study guide and organizational tool.
2	Student exhibited partial understanding of proper Foldables graphic organizer assembly. Student recorded most but not all information related to the chapter in the manner directed by the Foldables graphic organizer. Student demonstrated partial use of the Foldables graphic organizer as a study guide and organizational tool.
1	Student showed little understanding of proper Foldables graphic organizer assembly. Student recorded only some information related to the chapter in the manner directed by the Foldables graphic organizer. Student demonstrated little use of the Foldables graphic organizer as a study guide and organizational tool.
0	Student did not assemble Foldables graphic organizer according to instructions. Student recorded little or no information related to the chapter in the manner directed by the Foldables graphic organizer. Student did not use the Foldables graphic organizer as a study guide and organizational tool.

Name _____ Date _____

Chapter Test, Form 1

Read each question carefully. Write your answer on the line provided.

Add. Write each sum in simplest form.

1. $\frac{3}{6} + \frac{1}{6}$

   A. $\frac{1}{3}$ **B.** $\frac{2}{3}$ **C.** $\frac{3}{3}$ **D.** $\frac{4}{6}$ 1. _____

2. $\frac{2}{9} + \frac{1}{3}$

   F. $\frac{2}{3}$ **G.** $\frac{5}{9}$ **H.** $\frac{7}{9}$ **J.** $\frac{8}{9}$ 2. _____

Subtract. Write each difference in simplest form.

3. $\frac{7}{9} - \frac{2}{9}$

   A. $\frac{3}{9}$ **B.** $\frac{4}{9}$ **C.** $\frac{5}{9}$ **D.** $\frac{9}{9}$ 3. _____

4. $\frac{7}{8} - \frac{1}{2}$

   F. $\frac{1}{8}$ **G.** $\frac{2}{8}$ **H.** $\frac{3}{8}$ **J.** $\frac{1}{4}$ 4. _____

Solve.

5. A store sells $\frac{1}{3}$ pound of asparagus and $\frac{1}{2}$ pound of cabbage. How many pounds did the store sell altogether?

   A. $\frac{1}{2}$ **B.** $\frac{2}{3}$ **C.** $\frac{5}{6}$ **D.** $\frac{1}{3}$ 5. _____

6. Marya has $21.22 saved in the bank. She wants to buy a birthday present for her sister that costs $8.99, but she must keep $20.00 in the bank. How much more money does Marya need to save?

   F. $5.66   **G.** $6.77   **H.** $7.77   **J.** $7.99   6. _____

7. Polly spent $\frac{1}{6}$ hour reading a mystery and $\frac{2}{3}$ hour reading historical fiction. How many hours did Polly spend reading these two books?

   A. $\frac{2}{3}$ **B.** $\frac{5}{6}$ **C.** 1   **D.** $\frac{1}{3}$ 7. _____

Estimate by rounding each mixed number to the nearest whole number.

8. $3\frac{3}{5} + 1\frac{1}{5}$

   F. 4   **G.** 5   **H.** 6   **J.** 7   8. _____

9. $2\frac{5}{6} + 9\frac{2}{12}$

   A. 11   **B.** 12   **C.** 13   **D.** 14   9. _____

Subtract. Write each difference in simplest form.

10. $8\frac{3}{8} - 3\frac{1}{8}$

    F. $5\frac{1}{8}$ **G.** $5\frac{1}{4}$ **H.** $6\frac{1}{4}$ **J.** $6\frac{3}{4}$ 10. _____

11. $12\frac{9}{10} - 4\frac{1}{5}$

    A. $7\frac{1}{10}$ **B.** $8\frac{7}{10}$ **C.** $8\frac{1}{5}$ **D.** $7\frac{2}{10}$ 11. _____

12. $5\frac{2}{5} - 3\frac{1}{3}$

    F. $1\frac{3}{5}$ **G.** $1\frac{4}{5}$ **H.** $2\frac{1}{15}$ **J.** $2\frac{3}{5}$ 12. _____

13. $10\frac{5}{8} - 6\frac{7}{8}$

    A. $3\frac{1}{4}$ **B.** $3\frac{1}{2}$ **C.** $3\frac{3}{4}$ **D.** 4   13. _____

14. $9\frac{1}{4} - 4\frac{3}{4}$

    F. $3\frac{3}{4}$ **G.** 4   **H.** $4\frac{1}{4}$ **J.** $4\frac{1}{2}$ 14. _____

Assessment

Name _____ Date _____

Chapter Test, Form 2A

Read each question carefully. Write your answer on the line provided.

Add. Write each sum in simplest form.

1. $\frac{1}{6} + \frac{2}{6}$

   A. $\frac{1}{3}$ **B.** $\frac{1}{2}$ **C.** $\frac{2}{3}$ **D.** $\frac{5}{6}$ 1. _____

2. $\frac{1}{3} + \frac{4}{9}$

   F. $\frac{2}{3}$ **G.** $\frac{5}{9}$ **H.** $\frac{7}{9}$ **J.** $\frac{8}{9}$ 2. _____

Subtract. Write each difference in simplest form.

3. $\frac{2}{3} - \frac{2}{9}$

   A. $\frac{3}{9}$ **B.** $\frac{4}{9}$ **C.** $\frac{5}{9}$ **D.** $\frac{9}{9}$ 3. _____

4. $\frac{7}{8} - \frac{3}{8}$

   F. $\frac{1}{8}$ **G.** $\frac{2}{8}$ **H.** $\frac{3}{8}$ **J.** $\frac{1}{2}$ 4. _____

Solve.

5. A store sells $13\frac{2}{3}$ pounds of carrots and $4\frac{1}{3}$ pounds of celery. How many pounds did the store sell altogether?

   A. $17\frac{1}{2}$ **B.** 18   **C.** $18\frac{2}{3}$ **D.** $18\frac{3}{4}$ 5. _____

6. Renee has $12.56 saved in the bank. She wants to buy a birthday present for her brother that costs $2.99, but she must keep $15.00 in the bank. How much more money does Renee need to save?

   F. $5.43   **G.** $6.77   **H.** $7.77   **J.** $7.99   6. _____

7. Ivan spent $\frac{5}{6}$ hour reading a novel and $\frac{2}{3}$ hour reading magazines. How many hours did Ivan spend reading?

   A. 2   **B.** $1\frac{1}{2}$ **C.** 1   **D.** $\frac{1}{3}$ 7. _____

Estimate by rounding each mixed number to the nearest whole number.

8. $4\frac{1}{5} + 1\frac{1}{5}$

   F. 4   **G.** 5   **H.** 6   **J.** 7   8. _____

9. $1\frac{1}{6} + 10\frac{1}{6}$

   A. 11   **B.** 12   **C.** 13   **D.** 14   9. _____

Subtract. Write each difference in simplest form.

10. $6\frac{3}{8} - 2\frac{2}{16}$

   F. $4\frac{1}{4}$ **G.** $5\frac{1}{4}$ **H.** $6\frac{1}{4}$ **J.** $6\frac{3}{4}$ 10. _____

11. $12\frac{3}{5} - 3\frac{7}{10}$

   A. $7\frac{1}{10}$ **B.** $8\frac{1}{10}$ **C.** $8\frac{9}{10}$ **D.** $9\frac{2}{10}$ 11. _____

12. $5\frac{1}{5} - 2\frac{4}{5}$

   F. $1\frac{3}{5}$ **G.** $1\frac{4}{5}$ **H.** $2\frac{2}{5}$ **J.** $2\frac{3}{5}$ 12. _____

13. $8\frac{1}{2} - 6\frac{7}{8}$

   A. $1\frac{5}{8}$ **B.** $2\frac{6}{8}$ **C.** $3\frac{3}{4}$ **D.** 4   13. _____

14. $9\frac{3}{4} - 4\frac{3}{4}$

   F. $3\frac{3}{4}$ **G.** 4   **H.** $4\frac{1}{4}$ **J.** 5   14. _____

Name _____ Date _____

Read each question carefully. Write your answer on the line provided.

Add. Write each sum in simplest form.

1. $\frac{1}{9} + \frac{1}{6}$

   A. $\frac{1}{6}$ **B.** $\frac{5}{18}$ **C.** $\frac{2}{9}$ **D.** $\frac{1}{18}$ 1. _____

2. $\frac{4}{9} + \frac{2}{9}$

   F. $\frac{2}{3}$ **G.** $\frac{5}{9}$ **H.** $\frac{7}{9}$ **J.** $\frac{8}{9}$ 2. _____

Subtract. Write each difference in simplest form.

3. $\frac{5}{9} - \frac{1}{3}$

   A. $\frac{3}{9}$ **B.** $\frac{4}{9}$ **C.** $\frac{2}{9}$ **D.** $\frac{9}{9}$ 3. _____

4. $\frac{7}{8} - \frac{5}{8}$

   F. $\frac{1}{8}$ **G.** $\frac{2}{7}$ **H.** $\frac{3}{8}$ **J.** $\frac{1}{4}$ 4. _____

Solve.

5. A store sells $14\frac{2}{3}$ pounds of carrots one day. The next day the store sells $2\frac{1}{3}$ pounds of carrots. How many pounds of carrots did the store sell?

   A. 17   **B.** 18   **C.** $18\frac{2}{3}$ **D.** $18\frac{3}{4}$ 5. _____

6. Wanda has $11.56 saved in the bank. She wants to buy a gift that costs $1.99, but she must keep $10.00 in the bank. How much more money does Wanda need to save?

   F. $0.43   **G.** $0.77   **H.** $1.77   **J.** $1.99   6. _____

7. Ivan read for $\frac{1}{4}$ hour today. He read for $\frac{2}{3}$ hour yesterday. How many hours did Ivan read?

   A. $\frac{11}{12}$ **B.** $\frac{1}{12}$ **C.** $\frac{1}{4}$ **D.** $\frac{2}{7}$ 7. _____

Name _____ Date _____

Chapter Test, Form 2B *(continued)*

Estimate. Round to the nearest whole number.

8. $3\frac{1}{5} + 6\frac{1}{5}$

    F. 4   **G.** 5   **H.** 9   **J.** 10   **8.** _____

9. $3\frac{1}{6} + 5\frac{1}{6}$

    A. 8   **B.** 10   **C.** 11   **D.** 14   **9.** _____

Subtract. Write in simplest form.

10. $10\frac{3}{8} - 2\frac{1}{8}$

    F. $4\frac{1}{4}$ **G.** $5\frac{1}{4}$ **H.** $6\frac{1}{4}$ **J.** $8\frac{1}{4}$ **10.** _____

11. $12\frac{1}{5} - 3\frac{9}{10}$

    A. $7\frac{1}{10}$ **B.** $8\frac{3}{10}$ **C.** $8\frac{9}{10}$ **D.** $9\frac{2}{10}$ **11.** _____

12. $6\frac{1}{5} - 3\frac{4}{5}$

    F. $1\frac{3}{5}$ **G.** $1\frac{4}{5}$ **H.** $2\frac{2}{5}$ **J.** $2\frac{3}{5}$ **12.** _____

13. $5\frac{1}{8} - 2\frac{7}{8}$

    A. $1\frac{5}{8}$ **B.** $2\frac{1}{4}$ **C.** $3\frac{3}{4}$ **D.** 4   **13.** _____

14. $8\frac{3}{4} - 5\frac{3}{4}$

    F. 3   **G.** 4   **H.** $4\frac{1}{4}$ **J.** 5   **14.** _____

Name _____ Date _____

Chapter Test, Form 2C

Read each question carefully. Write your answer on the line provided.

Add. Write each sum in simplest form.

1. $\frac{3}{6} + \frac{1}{8}$

   A. $\frac{1}{8}$ B. $\frac{5}{8}$ C. $\frac{11}{24}$ D. $\frac{13}{24}$ 1. _____

2. $\frac{1}{9} + \frac{4}{9}$

   F. $\frac{2}{3}$ G. $\frac{5}{9}$ H. $\frac{7}{9}$ J. $\frac{8}{9}$ 2. _____

Subtract. Write each difference in simplest form.

3. $\frac{8}{9} - \frac{1}{3}$

   A. $\frac{3}{9}$ B. $\frac{4}{9}$ C. $\frac{5}{9}$ D. $\frac{9}{9}$ 3. _____

4. $\frac{6}{8} - \frac{3}{8}$

   F. $\frac{1}{8}$ G. $\frac{2}{8}$ H. $\frac{3}{8}$ J. $\frac{1}{2}$ 4. _____

Solve.

5. A store sells $\frac{3}{5}$ pound of carrots and $\frac{1}{3}$ pound of asparagus. How many pounds did the store sell altogether?

   A. $\frac{14}{15}$ B. $\frac{1}{15}$ C. $\frac{3}{5}$ D. $\frac{11}{15}$ 5. _____

6. Tom has $32.56 saved in the bank. He wants to buy a birthday present for his sister that costs $12.98, but he must keep $25.00 in the bank. How much more money does Tom need to save?

   F. $5.42   G. $6.77   H. $7.77   J. $7.99   6. _____

7. Annie spent $3\frac{1}{3}$ hours reading a novel and $1\frac{1}{3}$ hours reading poetry. How many hours did Annie spend reading?

   A. $3\frac{2}{3}$ B. $4\frac{2}{3}$ C. 5   D. $5\frac{1}{3}$ 7. _____

Estimate by rounding each mixed number to the nearest whole number.

8. $3\frac{2}{5} + 1\frac{1}{5}$

   F. 4   **G.** 5   **H.** 6   **J.** 7   8. _____

9. $1\frac{5}{6} + 10\frac{1}{6}$

   A. 11   **B.** 12   **C.** 13   **D.** 14   9. _____

Subtract. Write each difference in simplest form.

10. $6\frac{1}{8} - 2\frac{3}{8}$

   F. $3\frac{3}{4}$ **G.** $5\frac{1}{4}$ **H.** $6\frac{1}{4}$ **J.** $6\frac{3}{4}$ 10. _____

11. $2\frac{3}{5} - 1\frac{7}{10}$

   A. $\frac{8}{10}$ **B.** $\frac{9}{10}$ **C.** $1\frac{1}{10}$ **D.** $2\frac{2}{10}$ 11. _____

12. $4\frac{1}{5} - 1\frac{3}{5}$

   F. $1\frac{3}{5}$ **G.** $1\frac{4}{5}$ **H.** $2\frac{2}{5}$ **J.** $2\frac{3}{5}$ 12. _____

13. $4\frac{3}{8} - 2\frac{1}{4}$

   A. $1\frac{1}{2}$ **B.** $2\frac{1}{8}$ **C.** $3\frac{3}{4}$ **D.** 4   13. _____

14. $8\frac{1}{4} - 3\frac{3}{4}$

   F. $3\frac{3}{4}$ **G.** 4   **H.** $4\frac{1}{2}$ **J.** 5   14. _____

Assessment

10

Chapter Test, Form 2D

Read each question carefully. Write your answer on the line provided.

Add. Write in simplest form.

1. $\frac{2}{6} + \frac{1}{4}$

   A. $\frac{1}{3}$ B. $\frac{7}{12}$ C. $\frac{2}{3}$ D. $\frac{5}{6}$ 1. _____

2. $\frac{3}{9} + \frac{2}{9}$

   F. $\frac{2}{3}$ G. $\frac{5}{9}$ H. $\frac{7}{9}$ J. $\frac{8}{9}$ 2. _____

Subtract. Write in simplest form.

3. $\frac{4}{9} - \frac{2}{9}$

   A. $\frac{2}{9}$ B. $\frac{4}{9}$ C. $\frac{5}{9}$ D. $\frac{9}{9}$ 3. _____

4. $\frac{7}{8} - \frac{1}{2}$

   F. $\frac{1}{8}$ G. $\frac{2}{8}$ H. $\frac{3}{8}$ J. $\frac{1}{4}$ 4. _____

Solve.

5. A store sells $10\frac{1}{3}$ pounds of potatoes one day. The next day the store sells $2\frac{1}{3}$ pounds of potatoes. How many pounds of potatoes did the store sell?

   A. $12\frac{1}{3}$ B. $12\frac{2}{3}$ C. $13\frac{2}{3}$ D. $18\frac{3}{4}$ 5. _____

6. Charlie has $13.88 saved in the bank. He wants to buy a gift that costs $5.49, but he must keep $10.00 in the bank. How much more money does Charlie need to save?

   F. $0.63   G. $0.87   H. $1.61   J. $5.49   6. _____

7. Tammy read for $\frac{1}{3}$ hour today. She read for $\frac{1}{6}$ hour yesterday. How many hours did Tammy read?

   A. $\frac{1}{6}$ B. $\frac{1}{4}$ C. $\frac{1}{3}$ D. $\frac{1}{2}$ 7. _____

Grade 5

78

Chapter 10

Estimate. Round to the nearest whole number.

8. $2\frac{1}{5} + 5\frac{1}{5}$

   F. 4   **G.** 5   **H.** 7   **J.** 10   8. _____

9. $3\frac{5}{6} + 5\frac{10}{12}$

   A. 8   **B.** 10   **C.** 11   **D.** 14   9. _____

Subtract. Write in simplest form.

10. $10\frac{1}{8} - 2\frac{1}{4}$

    F. $4\frac{1}{4}$ **G.** $5\frac{1}{4}$ **H.** $6\frac{1}{4}$ **J.** $7\frac{7}{8}$ 10. _____

11. $7\frac{3}{10} - 3\frac{9}{10}$

    A. $3\frac{1}{10}$ **B.** $3\frac{1}{5}$ **C.** $3\frac{2}{5}$ **D.** $9\frac{3}{10}$ 11. _____

12. $4\frac{2}{5} - 3\frac{4}{5}$

    F. $\frac{3}{5}$ **G.** $\frac{4}{5}$ **H.** $1\frac{2}{5}$ **J.** $1\frac{3}{5}$ 12. _____

13. $7\frac{1}{4} - 2\frac{7}{8}$

    A. $1\frac{5}{8}$ **B.** $2\frac{1}{2}$ **C.** $3\frac{3}{4}$ **D.** $4\frac{3}{8}$ 13 _____

14. $9\frac{3}{4} - 6\frac{9}{12}$

    F. 3   **G.** 4   **H.** $4\frac{1}{4}$ **J.** 5   14. _____

Name _____ Date _____

Chapter Test, Form 3

Read each question carefully. Write your answer on the line provided.

Add. Write each sum in simplest form.

1. $\frac{5}{6} + \frac{1}{9}$

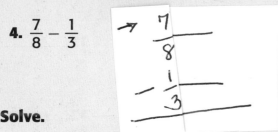

1. _____

2. $\frac{3}{9} + \frac{4}{9}$

2. _____

Subtract. Write each difference in simplest form.

3. $\frac{8}{12} - \frac{3}{12}$

3. _____

4. $\frac{7}{8} - \frac{1}{3}$

4. _____

Solve.

5. A store sells $15\frac{2}{3}$ pounds of carrots, $12\frac{1}{3}$ pounds of asparagus, and $3\frac{2}{3}$ pounds of cabbage. How many pounds did the store sell altogether?

5. _____

6. Tom has $36.56 saved in the bank. He wants to buy a birthday present for his sister that costs $12.98, and a present for his brother that costs $13.99. He must keep $25.00 in the bank. How much more money does Tom need to save?

6. _____

7. Amanda spent the weekend reading. On Friday night, she read for $\frac{1}{3}$ hour. On Saturday, she read for $\frac{1}{6}$ hour, and on Sunday she read for $\frac{1}{4}$ hour. How many hours did Amanda spend reading?

7. _____

Estimate by rounding each mixed number to the nearest whole number.

8. $3\frac{2}{5} + 1\frac{1}{5} + \frac{4}{5}$

8. _____

9. $1\frac{5}{6} + 10\frac{1}{6} + 5\frac{5}{6}$

9. _____

Subtract. Write each difference in simplest form.

10. $6\frac{2}{8} - 2\frac{7}{8}$

10. _____

11. $12\frac{3}{5} - 1\frac{7}{10}$

11. _____

12. $14\frac{1}{15} - 11\frac{4}{15}$

12. _____

13. $4\frac{1}{6} - 2\frac{7}{18}$

13. _____

14. $8\frac{1}{14} - 3\frac{3}{14}$

14. _____

10

Chapter Extended-Response Test

Demonstrate your knowledge by giving a clear, concise solution to each problem. Be sure to include all relevant drawings and justify your answers. You may show your solution in more than one way or investigate beyond the requirements of the problem. If necessary, record your answer on another piece of paper.

1. Explain in your own words what a fraction is. Draw a picture of a fraction. Explain your drawing.

2. There are 18 apples on the tree in the Donaldson's front yard. Patrick climbed the tree and ate 3 of the apples. Dawn shook the tree, and 2 more apples fell. What fraction of the apples is still on the tree?

   a. Explain in your own words what a numerator is. What is the numerator of the fraction of the apples that Patrick ate? What is the numerator of the fraction of the apples that fell to the ground?

   b. Explain in your own words what a denominator is. What is the denominator of the fraction of the apples that Patrick ate? What is the denominator of the fraction of the apples that fell to the ground?

   c. What is the fraction that represents the apples that are no longer in the tree?

3. What does it mean when a fraction is in simplest form?

   a. What is the simplest form of $\frac{2}{10}$?

   b. What is the simplest form of $\frac{4}{20}$?

   c. What is the simplest form of $\frac{3}{9}$?

   d. How do you know when a fraction is in simplest form?

4. What are equivalent fractions? Make up a problem using the apple tree in the Donaldson's yard that includes equivalent fractions.

Name _____ Date _____

Cumulative Test Practice Chapters 1–10

Test Example

Austin has completed $\frac{4}{12}$ of a group project. Ella has completed $\frac{4}{12}$ of the project. What portion of the project has been completed by the students?

A. $\frac{1}{6}$

B. $\frac{1}{4}$

C. $\frac{7}{12}$

D. $\frac{2}{3}$

Read the Test Item

You need to find the sum of $\frac{4}{12}$ and $\frac{4}{12}$.

Solve the Test Item

Use models to add the fractions.

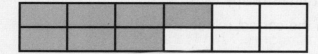 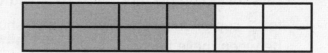

$$\frac{4}{12} + \frac{4}{12} = \frac{4+4}{12} = \frac{8}{12} = \frac{2}{3}$$

The answer is D.

Choose the best answer.

1. Nina at $\frac{1}{6}$ of a pie. Her two sisters each ate $\frac{2}{3}$ of the pie. How much of the pie did Nina and her sisters eat?

   A. $\frac{1}{3}$

   B. $\frac{5}{6}$

   C. $\frac{2}{3}$

   D. $\frac{3}{4}$

   1. _____

2. Julian had homework 3 out of 5 days last week. Which fraction is greater than $\frac{3}{5}$?

   F. $\frac{1}{8}$

   G. $\frac{1}{4}$

   H. $\frac{1}{2}$

   J. $\frac{4}{5}$

   2. _____

3. Hannah is making a quilt. She has completed 15 patches. If the quilt has 30 patches in all, what fraction of the quilt has Hannah completed?

   A. $\frac{1}{4}$ **B.** $\frac{1}{2}$ **C.** $\frac{1}{3}$ **D.** $\frac{3}{4}$ **3.** _____

4. What is the *x*-coordinate of point *L* shown below?

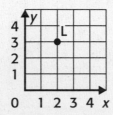

   F. (3, 5)   **G.** (5, 3)   **H.** (2, 3)   **J.** (5, 2)   **4.** _____

5. Inez and Christina are making chocolate chip cookies. Inez's recipe calls for $\frac{1}{4}$ cup of chips per dozen, and Christina's recipe calls for $\frac{3}{8}$ cup of chips per dozen. Which shows the correct relationship between these fractions?

   A. $\frac{1}{4} < \frac{3}{8}$ **B.** $\frac{3}{8} + \frac{1}{4}$ **C.** $\frac{1}{4} > \frac{3}{8}$ **D.** $\frac{1}{4} = \frac{3}{8}$ **5.** _____

6. Victor and his brothers bought a bag of oranges at the market. Victor has 3 brothers. If they ate $\frac{5}{8}$ of the oranges, what fraction of the oranges remained?

   F. $\frac{4}{8}$ **G.** $\frac{1}{2}$ **H.** $\frac{3}{8}$ **J.** $\frac{2}{3}$ **6.** _____

7. The graph shows some areas around Dominic's home town.

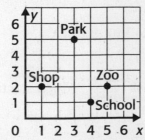

Which ordered pair best represents the point on the graph labeled "Zoo"?

   A. (2, 5)   **B.** (5, 2)   **C.** (1, 4)   **D.** (2, 3)   **7.** _____

8. Fiona measured the rainfall yesterday. In the morning, she collected $\frac{1}{5}$ inch of rainwater in her measuring cup and then emptied her cup. In the afternoon, she measured $\frac{3}{10}$ inch of rainwater. How much rainwater did she measure?

   F. $\frac{3}{10}$ inch   **H.** $\frac{4}{5}$ inch

   G. $\frac{1}{2}$ inch   **J.** $\frac{1}{3}$ inch

   8. _____

9. Jamal painted $\frac{2}{9}$ of his bedroom wall. His brother painted another $\frac{4}{9}$. How much of the wall is painted?

   9. _____

10. Lydia bought a bag of 12 apples to share with her family. If they ate 8 of the apples, what fraction of the apples did they eat?

    10. _____

11. Alana feeds her dog $\frac{2}{9}$ cup of food in the morning and $\frac{1}{3}$ cup in the evening. How much food does Alana's dog eat each day?

    11. _____

12. Mrs. Menendez made a pan of brownies. If there were 25 brownies in all and 15 of them were eaten, what fraction of the brownies was eaten?

    12. _____

13. Robert has finished $\frac{2}{3}$ of the book he is reading. His sister has finished $\frac{4}{10}$ of the book she is reading. Using >, <, or =, write an equation that shows the correct relationship between these fractions.

    13. _____

14. Gino ate 2 of the 12 pieces of fruit in the fruit basket. What fraction of the fruit did Gino eat?

    14. _____

Name _____ Date _____

Student Recording Sheet

Use this recording sheet with pages 470–471 of the Student Edition.

Read each question. Then fill in the correct answer.

1. Ⓐ Ⓑ Ⓒ Ⓓ

2. Ⓕ Ⓖ Ⓗ Ⓙ

3. Ⓐ Ⓑ Ⓒ Ⓓ

4. Ⓕ Ⓖ Ⓗ Ⓙ

5. Ⓐ Ⓑ Ⓒ Ⓓ

6. Ⓕ Ⓖ Ⓗ Ⓙ

7. Ⓐ Ⓑ Ⓒ Ⓓ

8. Ⓕ Ⓖ Ⓗ Ⓙ

9. Ⓐ Ⓑ Ⓒ Ⓓ

10. _____

11. _____

12. _____
_____
_____

13. _____
_____
_____

Answers (Graphic Organizer and Anticipation Guide)

Graphic Organizer (left page)

Name _____ Date _____

10 Graphic Organizer

Use this graphic organizer to take notes on **Chapter 10: Add and Subtract Fractions.**
Fill in the missing information.

Adding and Subtracting Like Fractions

○○○○● + ○○○○● =	Like fractions have the same **denominator**.
	Are these like fractions?
	Y or N **Y**
	What is the total of the two fractions? $\frac{3}{5}$
$\frac{2}{3} - \frac{1}{3} =$	$\frac{1}{3}$
If there are 8 apples altogether and one person eats 2 apples and another eats 1, how many of the 8 are left? How would you show this situation in an equation?	$\frac{2}{8} + \frac{1}{8} = \frac{3}{8}$ **There are 5 apples left.**
$\frac{3}{4} - \frac{1}{4} =$	$\frac{2}{4}$
	Is this fraction in its simplest form?
	Y or N **Y**
	If not, what is the simplified fraction? $\frac{1}{2}$

Anticipation Guide (right page)

Name _____ Date _____

Anticipation Guide
Add and Subtract Fractions

STEP 1   Before you begin Chapter 10

- Read each statement.
- Decide whether you agree (A) or disagree (D) with the statement.
- Write A or D in the first column OR if you are not sure whether you agree or disagree, write NS (not sure).

STEP 1 A, D, or NS	Statement	STEP 2 A or D
	1. Like fractions have the same denominator.	**A**
	2. Unlike fractions have the same numerator.	**D**
	3. $\frac{1}{7}$ and $\frac{6}{7}$ are like fractions.	**A**
	4. $\frac{13}{4}$ is a mixed number.	**D**
	5. $2\frac{1}{2}$ is an improper fraction.	**D**

STEP 2   After you complete Chapter 10

- Reread each statement and complete the last column by entering an A (agree) or a D (disagree).
- Did any of your opinions about the statements change from the first column?
- For those statements that you mark with a D, use a separate sheet of paper to explain why you disagree. Use examples, if possible.

Answers

Reteach

Name _____ Date _____

10–1

Add Like Fractions

Follow these steps to add fractions with like denominators.

Add $\frac{3}{8} + \frac{1}{8}$

Step 1

Add the numerators.
Use the like denominator.

$\frac{3}{8} + \frac{1}{8} = \frac{4}{8}$

So, $\frac{3}{8} + \frac{1}{8} = \frac{4}{8}$

Step 2

Write the sum in simplest form.
Divide the numerator and denominator by their greatest common factor.

$\frac{4}{8} = \frac{4 \div 4}{8 \div 4} = \frac{1}{2}$

Add. Write each sum in simplest form.

1. $\frac{5}{7} + \frac{4}{7} = \frac{9}{7}$ or $1\frac{2}{7}$
2. $\frac{1}{4} + \frac{1}{4} = \frac{1}{2}$
3. $\frac{3}{10} + \frac{1}{10} = \frac{2}{5}$
4. $\frac{7}{8} + \frac{5}{8} = 1\frac{1}{2}$
5. $\frac{11}{12} + \frac{7}{12} = 1\frac{1}{2}$
6. $\frac{3}{10} + \frac{2}{10} = \frac{1}{2}$
7. $\frac{1}{3} + \frac{3}{3} = 1\frac{1}{3}$
8. $\frac{1}{2} + \frac{3}{2} = 2$
9. $\frac{1}{9} + \frac{3}{9} = \frac{4}{9}$
10. $\frac{1}{7} + \frac{4}{7} = \frac{5}{7}$
11. $\frac{2}{10} + \frac{3}{10} = \frac{1}{2}$
12. $\frac{1}{6} + \frac{3}{6} = \frac{2}{3}$

Skills Practice

Name _____ Date _____

10–1

Add Like Fractions

Add. Write each in simplest form.

1. $\frac{7}{10} + \frac{1}{10} = \frac{4}{5}$
2. $\frac{13}{16} + \frac{7}{16} = 1\frac{1}{4}$
3. $\frac{4}{5} + \frac{1}{5} = 1$
4. $\frac{7}{12} + \frac{5}{12} = 1$
5. $\frac{4}{5} + \frac{3}{5} = 1\frac{2}{5}$
6. $\frac{5}{6} + \frac{5}{6} = 1\frac{2}{3}$
7. $\frac{7}{15} + \frac{2}{15} = \frac{3}{5}$
8. $\frac{9}{20} + \frac{3}{20} = \frac{3}{5}$
9. $\frac{1}{4} + \frac{1}{4} = \frac{1}{2}$
10. $\frac{3}{8} + \frac{1}{8} = \frac{1}{2}$
11. $\frac{2}{3} + \frac{1}{3} = 1$
12. $\frac{5}{6} + \frac{1}{6} = 1$
13. $\frac{7}{16} + \frac{3}{16} = \frac{5}{8}$
14. $\frac{3}{10} + \frac{9}{10} = 1\frac{1}{5}$
15. $\frac{7}{8} + \frac{7}{8} = 1\frac{3}{4}$
16. $\frac{7}{12} + \frac{11}{12} = 1\frac{1}{2}$
17. $\frac{19}{20} + \frac{5}{20} = 1\frac{1}{5}$
18. $\frac{11}{20} + \frac{7}{20} = \frac{9}{10}$
19. $\frac{9}{16} + \frac{7}{16} = 1$
20. $\frac{4}{5} + \frac{3}{5} = 1\frac{2}{5}$
21. $\frac{7}{9} + \frac{4}{9} = 1\frac{2}{9}$

Replace each  **with >, <, or = to make a true sentence.**

22. $\frac{7}{8} + \frac{5}{8}$ ⟨=⟩ $\frac{3}{4} + \frac{3}{4}$
23. $\frac{7}{10} + \frac{9}{10}$ ⟨>⟩ $\frac{3}{5} + \frac{4}{5}$
24. $\frac{2}{3} + \frac{2}{3}$ ⟨>⟩ $\frac{5}{12} + \frac{7}{12}$
25. $\frac{3}{8} + \frac{3}{8}$ ⟨<⟩ $\frac{9}{16} + \frac{5}{16}$
26. $\frac{3}{5} + \frac{3}{5}$ ⟨<⟩ $\frac{7}{10} + \frac{7}{10}$
27. $\frac{5}{8} + \frac{7}{8}$ ⟨=⟩ $\frac{13}{16} + \frac{11}{16}$

10–1

Name _____ Date _____

Homework Practice
Add Like Fractions

Add. Write each sum in simplest form.

1. $\frac{2}{5} + \frac{8}{5} = $ **2**
2. $\frac{5}{9} + \frac{1}{9} = $ **$\frac{2}{3}$**
3. $\frac{6}{8} + \frac{5}{8} = $ **$1\frac{3}{8}$**
4. $\frac{3}{4} + \frac{2}{4} = $ **$1\frac{1}{4}$**
5. $\frac{9}{9} + \frac{3}{9} = $ **$1\frac{1}{3}$**
6. $\frac{7}{8} + \frac{2}{8} = $ **$1\frac{1}{8}$**
7. $\frac{1}{2} + \frac{2}{2} = $ **$1\frac{1}{2}$**
8. $\frac{4}{5} + \frac{3}{5} = $ **$1\frac{2}{5}$**
9. $\frac{12}{15} + \frac{3}{15} = $ **1**
10. $\frac{6}{7} + \frac{1}{7} = $ **1**

11. Jasmine ate $\frac{3}{8}$ of a pizza. Manny ate $\frac{2}{8}$ of the same pizza. How much pizza did they eat altogether? Write a fraction in simplest form. **$\frac{5}{8}$**

12. Deanna walked $\frac{4}{15}$ of a mile. Abi walked $\frac{5}{15}$ of a mile. How far did they walk altogether? Write as a fraction in simplest form. **$\frac{3}{5}$**

Spiral Review

Replace each ◯ with <, >, or = to make a true statement. (Lesson 9–9)

13. $\frac{1}{4}$ ◯ $\frac{3}{8}$ (<)
14. $\frac{2}{3}$ ◯ $\frac{6}{9}$ (=)
15. $\frac{1}{2}$ ◯ $\frac{5}{9}$ (<)
16. $\frac{1}{5}$ ◯ $\frac{2}{7}$ (<)
17. $\frac{3}{4}$ ◯ $\frac{5}{8}$ (>)
18. $\frac{7}{12}$ ◯ $\frac{6}{13}$ (>)

10–1

Name _____ Date _____

Problem-Solving Practice
Add Like Fractions

Solve. Write your answer in simplest form.

1. Debbie helped her mother with the laundry. She did $\frac{1}{8}$ of it on Monday and another $\frac{3}{8}$ of it on Tuesday. What fraction of the laundry has she done? **$\frac{1}{2}$ of the laundry**

2. Laureano worked $\frac{1}{4}$ hour one day and $\frac{3}{4}$ hour the next day. How many hours did he work on the two days? **1 hour**

3. Mindy likes to order fresh meat and vegetable wraps from a local restaurant. One cook can roll $\frac{1}{3}$ wraps in 5 minutes. Another cook can roll $\frac{2}{3}$ wraps in the same amount of time. How many wraps can the two cooks prepare in 5 minutes? **1 wrap**

4. John went to a museum to see model trains. He saw $\frac{2}{5}$ mile of track on the first floor of the museum. He saw $\frac{4}{5}$ mile of track on the second floor. How much track did John see? **$1\frac{1}{5}$**

5. Sherry was in charge of distributing 250 food items that were donated to the local food pantry. On Monday she distributed 87 items. On Tuesday, she distributed 63 more items. Fifty more items were distributed on Wednesday. What fraction of the food items was distributed by the end of the day on Wednesday? **$\frac{4}{5}$ of the items**

6. Laura and her sister Katie swim every day. Laura can swim $\frac{3}{7}$ mile in 10 minutes. Katie can swim $\frac{2}{7}$ mile in the same amount of time. If they swim for 20 minutes and their speeds stay the same, how far do the sisters swim? **$1\frac{3}{7}$ mile**

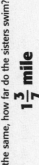
Answers

10–2 Reteach
Subtract Like Fractions

Follow these steps to subtract fractions with like denominators.

Subtract $\frac{8}{9} - \frac{2}{9}$

Step 1
Subtract the numerators.
Use the like denominator.

$\frac{8}{9} - \frac{2}{9} = \frac{6}{9}$

So, $\frac{8}{9} - \frac{2}{9} = \frac{6}{9} = \frac{2}{3}$

Step 2
Write the difference in simplest form.
Divide the numerator and denominator by their greatest common factor.

$\frac{6}{9} = \frac{6 \div 3}{9 \div 3} = \frac{2}{3}$

Subtract. Write each difference in simplest form.

1. $\frac{5}{7} - \frac{4}{7} = \frac{1}{7}$
2. $\frac{3}{4} - \frac{1}{4} = \frac{1}{2}$
3. $\frac{3}{10} - \frac{1}{10} = \frac{1}{5}$
4. $\frac{7}{8} - \frac{5}{8} = \frac{1}{4}$
5. $\frac{11}{12} - \frac{7}{12} = \frac{1}{3}$
6. $\frac{3}{10} - \frac{2}{10} = \frac{1}{10}$
7. $\frac{4}{6} - \frac{1}{6} = \frac{1}{2}$
8. $\frac{4}{3} - \frac{2}{3} = \frac{2}{3}$
9. $\frac{12}{9} - \frac{4}{9} = \frac{8}{9}$
10. $\frac{3}{2} - \frac{2}{2} = \frac{1}{2}$
11. $\frac{7}{8} - \frac{1}{8} = \frac{3}{4}$
12. $\frac{10}{10} - \frac{4}{10} = \frac{3}{5}$

10–1 Enrich
Fraction Pyramid!

In this triangle, the number in each blank circle is equal to the sum of the fractions in the two circles above it.

Add to find the missing fractions to complete the triangle.
Do not write your answers in simplest form.

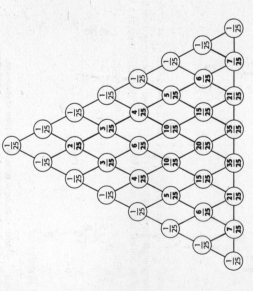

How many fractions less than 1 can you simplify in the triangle? **7**

Write the fractions in simplest form. $\frac{5}{25} = \frac{1}{5}; \frac{10}{25} = \frac{2}{5}; \frac{15}{25} = \frac{3}{5}; \frac{20}{25} = \frac{4}{5}$

How many fractions in the triangle are greater than 1? **2**

Write the fractions in simplest form. $\frac{35}{25} = 1\frac{2}{5}$

10-2 Skills Practice

Name _____ Date _____

Subtract Like Fractions

Subtract. Write each difference in simplest form.

1. $\dfrac{7}{10} - \dfrac{1}{10} = \dfrac{3}{5}$
2. $\dfrac{13}{16} - \dfrac{7}{16} = \dfrac{3}{8}$
3. $\dfrac{4}{5} - \dfrac{1}{5} = \dfrac{3}{5}$
4. $\dfrac{7}{12} - \dfrac{5}{12} = \dfrac{1}{6}$
5. $\dfrac{4}{5} - \dfrac{3}{5} = \dfrac{1}{5}$
6. $\dfrac{5}{6} - \dfrac{4}{6} = \dfrac{1}{6}$
7. $\dfrac{7}{15} - \dfrac{2}{15} = \dfrac{1}{3}$
8. $\dfrac{9}{20} - \dfrac{3}{20} = \dfrac{3}{10}$
9. $\dfrac{3}{8} - \dfrac{1}{8} = \dfrac{1}{4}$
10. $\dfrac{3}{8} - \dfrac{1}{8} = \dfrac{1}{4}$
11. $\dfrac{2}{3} - \dfrac{1}{3} = \dfrac{1}{3}$
12. $\dfrac{5}{6} - \dfrac{1}{6} = \dfrac{2}{3}$
13. $\dfrac{7}{16} - \dfrac{3}{16} = \dfrac{1}{4}$
14. $\dfrac{9}{10} - \dfrac{3}{10} = \dfrac{3}{5}$
15. $\dfrac{7}{8} - \dfrac{7}{8} = 0$
16. $\dfrac{11}{12} - \dfrac{7}{12} = \dfrac{1}{3}$
17. $\dfrac{19}{20} - \dfrac{5}{20} = \dfrac{7}{10}$
18. $\dfrac{11}{20} - \dfrac{7}{20} = \dfrac{1}{5}$
19. $\dfrac{9}{16} - \dfrac{7}{16} = \dfrac{1}{8}$
20. $\dfrac{4}{5} - \dfrac{3}{5} = \dfrac{1}{5}$

Replace each ◯ with >, <, or = to make a true sentence.

21. $\dfrac{7}{8} - \dfrac{5}{8}$ ⓥ $\dfrac{3}{4} - \dfrac{3}{4}$ → $>$
22. $\dfrac{9}{10} - \dfrac{7}{10}$ ⓥ $\dfrac{4}{5} - \dfrac{3}{5}$ → $=$
23. $\dfrac{2}{3} - \dfrac{1}{3}$ ⓥ $\dfrac{7}{12} - \dfrac{5}{12}$ → $>$
24. $\dfrac{3}{8} - \dfrac{3}{8}$ ⓥ $\dfrac{9}{16} - \dfrac{5}{16}$ → $<$
25. $\dfrac{5}{5} - \dfrac{3}{5}$ ⓥ $\dfrac{10}{10} - \dfrac{7}{10}$ → $>$
26. $\dfrac{7}{8} - \dfrac{5}{8}$ ⓥ $\dfrac{13}{16} - \dfrac{11}{16}$ → $>$

Grade 5 — 14 — Chapter 10

10-2 Homework Practice

Name _____ Date _____

Subtract Like Fractions

Subtract. Write each difference in simplest form.

1. $\dfrac{8}{5} - \dfrac{2}{5} = 1\dfrac{1}{5}$
2. $\dfrac{5}{9} - \dfrac{1}{9} = \dfrac{4}{9}$
3. $\dfrac{6}{8} - \dfrac{5}{8} = \dfrac{1}{8}$
4. $\dfrac{3}{4} - \dfrac{2}{4} = \dfrac{1}{4}$
5. $\dfrac{9}{9} - \dfrac{3}{9} = \dfrac{2}{3}$
6. $\dfrac{7}{8} - \dfrac{2}{8} = \dfrac{5}{8}$
7. $\dfrac{2}{2} - \dfrac{1}{2} = \dfrac{1}{2}$
8. $\dfrac{4}{5} - \dfrac{3}{5} = \dfrac{1}{5}$
9. $\dfrac{12}{15} - \dfrac{3}{15} = \dfrac{3}{5}$
10. $\dfrac{6}{7} - \dfrac{1}{7} = \dfrac{5}{7}$

Spiral Review

Add. Write each sum in simplest form. (Lesson 10–1)

11. $\dfrac{1}{9} + \dfrac{5}{9} = \dfrac{2}{3}$
12. $\dfrac{4}{6} + \dfrac{1}{6} = \dfrac{5}{6}$
13. $\dfrac{2}{3} + \dfrac{1}{3} = 1$
14. $\dfrac{7}{8} + \dfrac{2}{8} = \dfrac{9}{8}$ or $1\dfrac{1}{8}$
15. $\dfrac{2}{10} + \dfrac{1}{10} = \dfrac{3}{10}$
16. $\dfrac{1}{3} + \dfrac{6}{3} = \dfrac{7}{3}$ or $2\dfrac{1}{3}$
17. $\dfrac{5}{8} + \dfrac{3}{8} = \dfrac{8}{8}$ or 1
18. $\dfrac{5}{15} + \dfrac{5}{15} = \dfrac{2}{3}$
19. $\dfrac{7}{8} + \dfrac{1}{8} = \dfrac{8}{8}$ or 1
20. $\dfrac{2}{8} + \dfrac{5}{8} = \dfrac{7}{8}$
21. $\dfrac{5}{8} + \dfrac{11}{8} = 2$
22. $\dfrac{6}{7} + \dfrac{2}{7} = \dfrac{8}{7}$ or $1\dfrac{1}{7}$

Grade 5 — 15 — Chapter 10

Answers

Answers (Lesson 10–2)

10-2 Enrich

Name _____ Date _____

Fraction Puzzles

In the puzzles below, the sum of the fractions in each row is the same as the sum of the fractions in each column. Use your knowledge of adding and subtracting fractions to find the missing fractions. *Hint:* Remember to check the fractions for like denominators before adding.

$\frac{3}{20}$	$\frac{9}{20}$	$\frac{1}{20}$	$\frac{5}{20}$
$\frac{8}{20}$	$\frac{2}{20}$	$\frac{6}{20}$	$\frac{2}{20}$
$\frac{2}{20}$	$\frac{4}{20}$	$\frac{5}{20}$	$\frac{7}{20}$
$\frac{5}{20}$	$\frac{3}{20}$	$\frac{6}{20}$	$\frac{4}{20}$

$\frac{6}{25}$	$\frac{3}{25}$	$\frac{11}{25}$	$\frac{0}{25}$
$\frac{9}{25}$	$\frac{6}{25}$	$\frac{3}{25}$	$\frac{2}{25}$
$\frac{2}{25}$	$\frac{7}{25}$	$\frac{5}{25}$	$\frac{6}{25}$
$\frac{3}{25}$	$\frac{4}{25}$	$\frac{1}{25}$	$\frac{12}{25}$

$\frac{9}{15}$	$\frac{2}{15}$	$\frac{3}{15}$	$\frac{2}{15}$
$\frac{4}{15}$	$\frac{8}{15}$	$\frac{0}{15}$	$\frac{4}{15}$
$\frac{2}{15}$	$\frac{4}{15}$	$\frac{7}{15}$	$\frac{3}{15}$
$\frac{1}{15}$	$\frac{2}{15}$	$\frac{6}{15}$	$\frac{7}{15}$

$\frac{8}{16}$	$\frac{1}{16}$	$\frac{2}{16}$	$\frac{2}{16}$
$\frac{1}{16}$	$\frac{7}{16}$	$\frac{2}{16}$	$\frac{2}{16}$
$\frac{3}{16}$	$\frac{2}{16}$	$\frac{5}{16}$	$\frac{2}{16}$
$\frac{0}{16}$	$\frac{4}{16}$	$\frac{4}{16}$	$\frac{6}{16}$

CHALLENGE Create your own fraction puzzle using a box of 5 rows and 5 columns.

Grade 5   17

10-2 Problem-Solving Practice

Name _____ Date _____

Subtract Like Fractions

Solve. Write your answer in simplest form.

1. Beth bought $\frac{5}{6}$ pound of provolone cheese and $\frac{3}{6}$ pound of mozzarella cheese. How much more provolone than mozzarella did she buy?

   $\frac{1}{3}$ pound

2. An aquarium was $\frac{9}{10}$ full with water. After cleaning the aquarium, it was $\frac{4}{10}$ full with water. What fraction of the water was drained while cleaning the aquarium?

   $\frac{1}{2}$

3. On a class trip to the museum, $\frac{5}{8}$ of the students saw the dinosaurs and $\frac{2}{8}$ of the students saw the jewelry collection. What fraction of students saw the dinosaurs over the jewelry collection?

   $\frac{3}{8}$

4. At a family reunion, $\frac{7}{12}$ of Vanessa's family brought a dinner item and $\frac{5}{12}$ brought a dessert item. What part of her family brought dinner over dessert?

   $\frac{1}{6}$

5. Julio read $\frac{5}{9}$ of a book the first week and $\frac{2}{9}$ of the same book the second week. How much of the book did he have left to read?

   $\frac{2}{9}$ of the book

6. Brad completed $\frac{3}{10}$ of his homework immediately after school and $\frac{5}{10}$ of his homework after dinner. How much of his homework does he have left to do?

   $\frac{1}{5}$ of his homework

Grade 5   16

Answers (Lesson 10–3)

10–3 Reteach
Add Fractions with Unlike Denominators

Name _____ Date _____

When adding fractions with unlike denominators, it helps to write the problems in vertical form.

Add $\frac{7}{8} + \frac{2}{3}$

Step 1
Find the least common denominator (LCD).

Multiples of 3: 3, 6, 9, 12, 15, 18, 21, 24, …

Multiples of 8: 8, 16, **24**, …

The LCD is 24.

Step 2
Rename each fraction using the LCD.

$\frac{7}{8} = \frac{21}{24}$

$\frac{2}{3} = \frac{16}{24}$

Step 3
Write the problems in vertical form.

Add.

$$\begin{aligned}\frac{7}{8} &= \frac{21}{24}\\[-2pt]+\ \frac{2}{3} &= \frac{16}{24}\\ \hline &\ \ \frac{37}{24} = 1\frac{13}{24}\end{aligned}$$

Add. Write your answer in simplest form.

1. $\frac{3}{8} + \frac{5}{6}$

Multiples of 8: **8, 16, 24, 32, …**
Multiples of 6: **6, 12, 18, 24, …**
LCD: **24**
So, $\frac{3}{8} + \frac{5}{6} = \frac{9}{24} + \frac{20}{24} = \frac{29}{24} = 1\frac{5}{24}$

2. $\frac{11}{12} + \frac{3}{4}$

Multiples of 12: **12, 24, 36, …**
Multiples of 4: **4, 8, 12, …**
LCD: **12**
So, $\frac{11}{12} + \frac{3}{4} = \frac{11}{12} + \frac{9}{12} = \frac{20}{12} = 1\frac{2}{3}$

3. $\frac{4}{5} + \frac{2}{3} = 1\frac{7}{15}$

4. $\frac{3}{5} + \frac{9}{10} = \frac{15}{10} = 1\frac{1}{2}$

5. $\frac{9}{10} + \frac{5}{6} = 1\frac{11}{15}$

6. $\frac{7}{10} + \frac{3}{4} = 1\frac{9}{20}$

7. $\frac{5}{8} + \frac{2}{5} = \frac{1}{40} = 1\frac{1}{40}$

8. $\frac{3}{4} + \frac{5}{6} = 1\frac{7}{12}$

9. $\frac{1}{2} + \frac{3}{8} = \frac{7}{8}$

10. $\frac{1}{4} + \frac{3}{8} = \frac{5}{8}$

11. $\frac{3}{5} + \frac{3}{4} = \frac{27}{20} = 1\frac{7}{20}$

12. $\frac{7}{12} + \frac{1}{3} = \frac{11}{12}$

13. $\frac{5}{6} + \frac{5}{8} = \frac{35}{24} = 1\frac{11}{24}$

14. $\frac{7}{10} + \frac{2}{5} = 1\frac{1}{10}$

10–3 Skills Practice
Add Fractions with Unlike Denominators

Name _____ Date _____

Add. Write your answer in simplest form.

1. $\frac{1}{2} + \frac{1}{5} = \frac{7}{10}$

2. $\frac{2}{5} + \frac{7}{10} = 1\frac{1}{10}$

3. $\frac{5}{8} + \frac{3}{16} = \frac{13}{16}$

4. $\frac{3}{5} + \frac{3}{20} = \frac{3}{4}$

5. $\frac{9}{10} + \frac{7}{10} = 1\frac{3}{5}$

6. $\frac{7}{12} + \frac{1}{3} = \frac{11}{12}$

7. $\frac{9}{10} + \frac{2}{5} = 1\frac{3}{10}$

8. $\frac{3}{16} + \frac{3}{8} = \frac{9}{16}$

9. $\frac{3}{4} + \frac{2}{5} = 1\frac{3}{20}$

10. $\frac{7}{12} + \frac{3}{4} = 1\frac{1}{3}$

11. $\frac{2}{3} + \frac{3}{8} = 1\frac{1}{24}$

12. $\frac{9}{20} + \frac{3}{5} = 1\frac{1}{20}$

13. $\frac{7}{16} + \frac{3}{8} = \frac{13}{16}$

14. $\frac{5}{6} + \frac{7}{12} = 1\frac{5}{12}$

15. $\frac{15}{16} + \frac{5}{8} = 1\frac{9}{16}$

16. $\frac{17}{20} + \frac{3}{4} = 1\frac{3}{5}$

17. $\frac{1}{4} + \frac{4}{5} = 1\frac{1}{20}$

18. $\frac{1}{2} + \frac{1}{5} = \frac{7}{10}$

19. $\frac{5}{8} + \frac{2}{5} = 1\frac{1}{40}$

20. $\frac{7}{10} + \frac{1}{2} = 1\frac{1}{5}$

21. $\frac{5}{6} + \frac{5}{8} = 1\frac{11}{24}$

22. $\frac{5}{8} + \frac{3}{4} = 1\frac{3}{8}$

23. $\frac{3}{5} + \frac{1}{4} = \frac{17}{20}$

24. $\frac{5}{6} + \frac{7}{9} = 1\frac{11}{18}$

25. $\frac{9}{10} + \frac{7}{20} = 1\frac{1}{4}$

26. $\frac{3}{5} + \frac{5}{6} = 1\frac{13}{30}$

27. $\frac{5}{8} + \frac{35}{12} = 3\frac{13}{24}$

Problem Solving
Solve.

28. After school, Michael walks $\frac{3}{5}$ mile to the park and then walks $\frac{3}{4}$ mile to his house. How far does Michael walk from school to his house?

$1\frac{7}{20}$ **miles**

29. When Rachel walks to school on the sidewalk, she walks $\frac{7}{10}$ mile. When she takes the shortcut across the field, she walks $\frac{1}{4}$ mile less. How long is the shorter route?

$\frac{9}{20}$ **mile**

Answers (Lesson 10–3)

10-3

Name _____ **Date** _____

Problem-Solving Practice
Add Fractions with Unlike Denominators

Solve. Write your answer in simplest form.

1. Elizabeth made an English muffin pizza using $\frac{1}{4}$ cup of cheese and $\frac{1}{10}$ cup of sausage. How many cups of toppings did she use?

   $\frac{7}{20}$ **cups**

2. Eric delivers $\frac{1}{5}$ of the newspapers in the neighborhood, and Anita delivers $\frac{1}{2}$ of them. Eric and Anita deliver what fraction of the papers?

   $\frac{7}{10}$ **of the papers**

Solve. Write your answer in simplest form.

3. Christie took a social studies test on Monday. Two-fifths of the questions were multiple-choice, and $\frac{3}{7}$ of the question were true-false questions. What part of the total number of questions are either multiple choice or true-false questions?

   $\frac{29}{35}$

4. Brian was hungry and wanted to eat $\frac{3}{8}$ of a pie. His friend was even hungrier and wanted to eat $\frac{4}{5}$ of a pie. Will one pie be enough for the two boys? If not, how much of another pie is needed?

   No; $\frac{1}{8}$ **pie**

Solve. Write your answer in simplest form.

5. Sue took a survey in the fifth grade and found that $\frac{1}{4}$ of the students wore sandals, $\frac{4}{7}$ wore tennis shoes, and $\frac{1}{8}$ wore loafers. What part of the students wore one of these three types of shoes?

   $\frac{53}{56}$

6. Long's car is being repaired. His brother takes him where he needs to go from 9:00 A.M. to noon. His sister takes him where he needs to go from 2:00 P.M. to 7:00 P.M. Change these time periods to fractions of a day. In simplest terms, what part of the day does he have transportation to take him where he needs to go?

   $\frac{1}{3}$ **of the day**

Grade 5   21   *Chapter 10*

10-3

Name _____ **Date** _____

Homework Practice
Add Fractions with Unlike Denominators

Add. Write your answer in simplest form.

1. $\frac{2}{3}$
   $+\frac{3}{5}$
   $\overline{1\frac{4}{15}}$

2. $\frac{2}{3}$
   $+\frac{5}{9}$
   $\overline{1\frac{2}{9}}$

3. $\frac{3}{4}$
   $+\frac{5}{8}$
   $\overline{1\frac{3}{8}}$

4. $\frac{2}{7}$
   $+\frac{5}{14}$
   $\overline{\frac{9}{14}}$

5. $\frac{1}{2}$
   $+\frac{5}{6}$
   $\overline{1\frac{1}{3}}$

6. $\frac{11}{12}$
   $+\frac{3}{4}$
   $\overline{1\frac{2}{3}}$

7. $\frac{5}{12}$
   $+\frac{7}{15}$
   $\overline{\frac{9}{10}}$

8. $\frac{7}{15}$
   $+\frac{1}{6}$
   $\overline{\frac{19}{30}}$

9. $\frac{8}{9}$
   $+\frac{2}{3}$
   $\overline{1\frac{5}{9}}$

10. $\frac{5}{6}$
    $+\frac{3}{8}$
    $\overline{1\frac{5}{24}}$

11. $\frac{7}{15}$
    $+\frac{1}{3}$
    $\overline{\frac{4}{5}}$

12. $\frac{3}{4}$
    $+\frac{3}{10}$
    $\overline{1\frac{1}{20}}$

13. $\frac{2}{9}$
    $+\frac{5}{6}$
    $\overline{1\frac{1}{18}}$

14. $\frac{4}{5}$
    $+\frac{3}{4}$
    $\overline{1\frac{11}{20}}$

15. $\frac{11}{12}$
    $+\frac{7}{8}$
    $\overline{1\frac{19}{24}}$

16. $\frac{7}{10}$
    $+\frac{1}{6}$
    $\overline{\frac{13}{15}}$

17. $\frac{7}{8}$
    $+\frac{2}{3}$
    $\overline{1\frac{13}{14}}$

18. $\frac{9}{10}$
    $+\frac{9}{15}$
    $\overline{1\frac{1}{2}}$

19. $\frac{2}{5}+\frac{7}{10}=1\frac{1}{10}$

20. $\frac{5}{6}+\frac{4}{9}=1\frac{5}{18}$

21. $\frac{2}{3}+\frac{1}{4}=\frac{11}{12}$

22. $\frac{7}{10}+\frac{1}{5}=\frac{9}{10}$

23. $\frac{3}{4}+\frac{1}{3}=1\frac{1}{12}$

24. $\frac{5}{6}+\frac{2}{9}=1\frac{1}{18}$

25. $\frac{2}{5}+\frac{3}{10}=\frac{7}{10}$

26. $\frac{3}{4}+\frac{2}{3}=1\frac{5}{12}$

27. $\frac{3}{10}+\frac{3}{4}=1\frac{1}{20}$

Spiral Review

Solve.

28. Cathy spent $\frac{2}{5}$ of an hour on her French assignment and $\frac{4}{5}$ of an hour on her English report. How much more time did she spend on her English report than her French assignment? Write your answer in simplest form.

    $\frac{2}{5}$ **hour**

29. On saturday, Jason spent $\frac{9}{10}$ of his time skateboarding and $\frac{1}{10}$ of his time reading. How much more time did Jason spend skateboarding than reading?

    $\frac{4}{5}$

Grade 5   20   *Chapter 10*

10-4 Reteach

Name _____ Date _____

Subtract Unlike Fractions

You can draw models to help subtract fractions with unlike denominators.

Subtract $\dfrac{3}{4} - \dfrac{1}{3}$.

Show models for $\dfrac{3}{4}$ and $\dfrac{1}{3}$.

Find the LCD of $\dfrac{3}{4}$ and $\dfrac{1}{3}$.

Multiples of 4: 4, 8, **12**, ...
Multiples of 3: 3, 6, 9, **12**, ...
The LCD of $\dfrac{3}{4}$ and $\dfrac{1}{3}$ is 12.

Use models to show how many twelfths are in $\dfrac{3}{4}$, and how many twelfths are in $\dfrac{1}{3}$.

$$\dfrac{3}{4} \rightarrow \dfrac{9}{12}$$
$$\dfrac{1}{3} \rightarrow \dfrac{4}{12}$$

Take away models to subtract $\dfrac{4}{12}$.

$$\dfrac{3}{4} - \dfrac{1}{3} \rightarrow \dfrac{9}{12} - \dfrac{4}{12} = \dfrac{5}{12}$$

So, $\dfrac{3}{4} - \dfrac{1}{3} = \dfrac{5}{12}$.

Use the fraction models to subtract the fractions. Write your answer in simplest form.

1. $\dfrac{3}{4} - \dfrac{5}{12} \rightarrow \dfrac{9}{12} - \dfrac{5}{12} = \dfrac{1}{3}$

2. $\dfrac{1}{2}$

3. $\dfrac{9}{10} - \dfrac{3}{5} \rightarrow \dfrac{9}{10} - \dfrac{6}{10} = \dfrac{3}{10}$

$\dfrac{1}{2} - \dfrac{2}{5} \rightarrow \dfrac{5}{10} - \dfrac{4}{10} = \dfrac{1}{10}$

Subtract. You may use models. Write your answer in simplest form.

4. $\dfrac{1}{2} - \dfrac{3}{8} = \dfrac{1}{8}$

5. $\dfrac{5}{6} - \dfrac{7}{12} = \dfrac{1}{4}$

6. $\dfrac{11}{12} - \dfrac{1}{4} = \dfrac{2}{3}$

7. $\dfrac{2}{3} - \dfrac{1}{2} = \dfrac{1}{6}$

8. $\dfrac{9}{20} - \dfrac{2}{5} = \dfrac{1}{20}$

9. $\dfrac{7}{8} - \dfrac{1}{3} = \dfrac{13}{24}$

10-3 Enrich

Name _____ Date _____

Add Unlike Fractions

The fractions in the squares are addends. Write the pair of addends that will give each sum.

| $\dfrac{2}{3}$ | $\dfrac{3}{5}$ | $\dfrac{3}{8}$ | $\dfrac{1}{12}$ |

| $\dfrac{3}{4}$ | $\dfrac{7}{10}$ | $\dfrac{2}{5}$ | $\dfrac{5}{6}$ |

| $\dfrac{1}{16}$ | $\dfrac{7}{8}$ |

1. $\dfrac{3}{5} + \dfrac{7}{10} = 1\dfrac{3}{10}$

2. $\dfrac{2}{5} + \dfrac{7}{8} = 1\dfrac{11}{40}$

3. $\dfrac{2}{3} + \dfrac{3}{4} = 1\dfrac{5}{12}$

4. $\dfrac{1}{16} + \dfrac{7}{8} = \dfrac{15}{16}$

5. $\dfrac{3}{5} + \dfrac{3}{4} = 1\dfrac{7}{20}$

6. $\dfrac{7}{8} + \dfrac{1}{12} = \dfrac{23}{24}$

7. $\dfrac{2}{5} + \dfrac{2}{3} = 1\dfrac{1}{15}$

8. $\dfrac{1}{16} + \dfrac{3}{8} = \dfrac{7}{16}$

9. $\dfrac{1}{12} + \dfrac{5}{6} = \dfrac{11}{12}$

10. $\dfrac{7}{10} + \dfrac{2}{3} = 1\dfrac{11}{30}$

Answers

Answers (Lesson 10–4)

Skills Practice (10-4)

Name _____ Date _____

Skills Practice

Subtract Unlike Fractions

Write the subtraction sentence shown by each model. Write the difference in simplest form.

1. $\dfrac{3}{5} - \dfrac{3}{10} = \dfrac{3}{10}$
2. $\dfrac{2}{3} - \dfrac{1}{6} = \dfrac{1}{2}$
3. $\dfrac{3}{4} - \dfrac{4}{12} = \dfrac{5}{12}$
4. $\dfrac{1}{2} - \dfrac{1}{5} = \dfrac{3}{10}$
5. $\dfrac{3}{8} - \dfrac{4}{24} = \dfrac{5}{24}$
6. $\dfrac{5}{6} - \dfrac{3}{8} = \dfrac{11}{24}$

Subtract. Write your answer in simplest form.

7. $\dfrac{7}{12} - \dfrac{1}{4} = \dfrac{1}{3}$
8. $\dfrac{1}{2} - \dfrac{1}{3} = \dfrac{1}{6}$
9. $\dfrac{9}{10} - \dfrac{2}{5} = \dfrac{1}{2}$
10. $\dfrac{5}{8} - \dfrac{1}{4} = \dfrac{3}{8}$
11. $\dfrac{11}{20} - \dfrac{3}{10} = \dfrac{1}{4}$
12. $\dfrac{11}{12} - \dfrac{1}{3} = \dfrac{7}{12}$
13. $\dfrac{7}{10} - \dfrac{1}{2} = \dfrac{1}{5}$
14. $\dfrac{3}{4} - \dfrac{2}{3} = \dfrac{1}{12}$
15. $\dfrac{5}{6} - \dfrac{3}{4} = \dfrac{1}{12}$
16. $\dfrac{3}{4} - \dfrac{3}{5} = \dfrac{3}{20}$
17. $\dfrac{11}{12} - \dfrac{1}{4} = \dfrac{2}{3}$
18. $\dfrac{4}{5} - \dfrac{1}{2} = \dfrac{3}{10}$

Problem Solving

Solve.

19. The distance around a lily pond is $\dfrac{7}{10}$ mile. Rocks have been placed for $\dfrac{1}{4}$ mile along the pond's edge. How much of the edge does not have rocks? **$\dfrac{9}{20}$ mile**

20. The first $\dfrac{1}{5}$ mile of a $\dfrac{3}{4}$ mile path through a rose garden is paved with bricks. How much of the path is not paved with bricks? **$\dfrac{11}{20}$ mile**

Homework Practice (10-4)

Name _____ Date _____

Homework Practice

Subtract Unlike Fractions

Subtract. Write your answer in simplest form.

1. $\dfrac{2}{3} - \dfrac{3}{5} = \dfrac{1}{15}$
2. $\dfrac{2}{3} - \dfrac{5}{9} = \dfrac{1}{9}$
3. $\dfrac{3}{4} - \dfrac{5}{8} = \dfrac{1}{8}$
4. $\dfrac{5}{7} - \dfrac{5}{14} = \dfrac{5}{14}$
5. $\dfrac{1}{2} - \dfrac{1}{6} = \dfrac{1}{3}$
6. $\dfrac{11}{12} - \dfrac{3}{4} = \dfrac{1}{6}$
7. $\dfrac{5}{12} - \dfrac{1}{4} = \dfrac{1}{6}$
8. $\dfrac{7}{15} - \dfrac{1}{6} = \dfrac{3}{10}$
9. $\dfrac{8}{9} - \dfrac{2}{3} = \dfrac{2}{9}$
10. $\dfrac{5}{6} - \dfrac{3}{8} = \dfrac{11}{24}$
11. $\dfrac{7}{15} - \dfrac{1}{3} = \dfrac{2}{15}$
12. $\dfrac{3}{4} - \dfrac{4}{10} = \dfrac{7}{20}$
13. $\dfrac{8}{9} - \dfrac{5}{6} = \dfrac{1}{18}$
14. $\dfrac{4}{5} - \dfrac{3}{4} = \dfrac{1}{20}$
15. $\dfrac{11}{12} - \dfrac{7}{8} = \dfrac{1}{24}$
16. $\dfrac{7}{10} - \dfrac{1}{6} = \dfrac{8}{15}$
17. $\dfrac{7}{4} - \dfrac{5}{8} = \dfrac{9}{8}$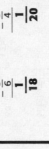
18. $\dfrac{9}{10} - \dfrac{9}{15} = \dfrac{3}{10}$
19. $\dfrac{4}{5} - \dfrac{7}{10} = \dfrac{1}{10}$
20. $\dfrac{5}{6} - \dfrac{4}{9} = \dfrac{7}{18}$
21. $\dfrac{2}{3} - \dfrac{1}{4} = \dfrac{5}{12}$
22. $\dfrac{7}{10} - \dfrac{1}{5} = \dfrac{1}{2}$
23. $\dfrac{3}{4} - \dfrac{1}{3} = \dfrac{5}{12}$
24. $\dfrac{5}{6} - \dfrac{2}{9} = \dfrac{11}{8}$
25. $\dfrac{2}{5} - \dfrac{1}{3} = \dfrac{7}{30}$
26. $\dfrac{3}{4} - \dfrac{2}{3} = \dfrac{1}{12}$
27. $\dfrac{9}{10} - \dfrac{3}{4} = \dfrac{3}{20}$

Spiral Review

Solve.

28. Clifton spent $\dfrac{2}{3}$ hour practicing guitar. He spent $\dfrac{1}{6}$ hour changing the strings on his guitar. How much time did he spend practicing and changing the strings? **$\dfrac{5}{6}$**

29. In the new den, $\dfrac{1}{6}$ of the walls will be made of glass blocks, and $\dfrac{1}{8}$ will be covered with tile. What fraction of the room will be covered with glass blocks and tile? **$\dfrac{7}{24}$**

Answers (Lesson 10–4)

Answers

Chapter Resources

Copyright © Macmillan/McGraw-Hill, a division of The McGraw-Hill Companies, Inc.

10–4

Name _____ Date _____

Problem-Solving Practice

Subtract Fractions with Unlike Denominators

Solve. Write your answer in simplest form.

1. Steve watched television for $\frac{3}{4}$ hour on Monday and $\frac{5}{6}$ hour on Tuesday. How many more hours did he watch television on Tuesday?

$\frac{1}{12}$ hour

2. Deanna uses $\frac{2}{3}$ cup flour and $\frac{1}{4}$ cup shortening in a recipe. How much more flour than shortening does she use?

$\frac{5}{12}$ cup

Solve. Write your answer in simplest form.

3. Marsha and her friend, Tina, are making table decorations for a party. Marsha made $\frac{2}{9}$ of a decoration in half an hour. Tina can make $\frac{2}{3}$ of a decoration in the same amount of time. How much more of a decoration can Tina make in half an hour?

$\frac{4}{9}$ decoration

4. Kyle planted flowers in the front of the school. He planted $\frac{1}{16}$ of the plants on Friday and $\frac{1}{4}$ of the plants on Saturday. On which day did he plant more flowers? What is the difference in the amount of flowers he planted on the two days?

Friday: $\frac{7}{16}$

Solve. Write your answer in simplest form.

5. Shawn rides his bicycle $\frac{9}{10}$ mile to school. On his way to school, he stops at Mike's house, which is $\frac{1}{5}$ mile from Shawn's house. Then they both ride to Jose's house, which is $\frac{2}{7}$ mile from Mike's house. How far is it from Jose's house to the school?

$\frac{29}{70}$ mile

6. After school, Laura babysits one child for 50 minutes. They rest for 10 minutes, read for 15 minutes, and play for the rest of the time. Write the total babysitting time, the resting time, and the reading time, as fractions of an hour.

$\frac{5}{6}$ hour babysitting; $\frac{1}{6}$ hour resting; $\frac{1}{4}$ hour reading

Use these fractions to find the fraction of an hour they play.

$\frac{5}{12}$ hour playing

Grade 5

Chapter 10

10–4

Name _____ Date _____

Enrich

Subtract Fractions with Unlike Denominators

Play "Five-in-a-Row" with a partner. You will need a coin.

- Player 1 selects any two fractions on the game board. Then the player tosses the coin. If the coin lands heads up, the player finds the sum of the fractions. If the coin lands tails up, the player finds the difference.

- Player 2 checks Player 1's sum or difference. If it is correct, Player 1 writes an X in each box containing the fractions added or subtracted

- Player 2 takes a turn and writes an O in each box.

- The player who marks five Xs or five Os in row wins. If no more boxes can be marked, the player who marked more boxes is the winner.

$\frac{1}{10}$	$\frac{3}{5}$	$\frac{7}{8}$	$\frac{1}{4}$	$\frac{4}{5}$
$\frac{3}{4}$	$\frac{1}{2}$	$\frac{5}{12}$	$\frac{1}{8}$	$\frac{7}{20}$
$\frac{5}{6}$	$\frac{3}{8}$	$\frac{1}{6}$	$\frac{3}{10}$	$\frac{1}{5}$
$\frac{1}{12}$	$\frac{2}{3}$	$\frac{2}{5}$	$\frac{5}{6}$	$\frac{1}{2}$
$\frac{5}{8}$	$\frac{1}{4}$	$\frac{7}{10}$	$\frac{3}{8}$	$\frac{1}{3}$

Grade 5

Chapter 10

Copyright © Macmillan/McGraw-Hill, a division of The McGraw-Hill Companies, Inc.

Grade 5

A11

Chapter 10

Answers (Lesson 10–5)

Name _____ Date _____

10-5 Reteach

Problem-Solving Strategy: Determine Reasonable Answers

Solve. Determine which answer is reasonable.

1. Renata bought 0.85 pound of pine nuts and 0.9 pound of macadamia nuts. Is 1.5 pounds, 2 pounds, or 2.5 pounds a more reasonable estimate for how many pounds of nuts she purchased altogether?

   2 pounds

2. One container has $2\frac{5}{8}$ pounds of pineapple and another has $1\frac{7}{8}$ pounds of pineapple. Sam buys both containers. Which is a more reasonable estimate for how many pounds of pineapple he bought in all: 4 pounds, 5 pounds, or 6 pounds?

   5 pounds

3. From the beginning of a trail, Claire hiked $4\frac{3}{8}$ miles to the lake. Then she hiked $2\frac{5}{8}$ miles to the nature center. Is 5 miles, 6 miles, or 7 miles a more reasonable estimate for how far Claire hiked altogether?

   7 miles

4. At the beginning of the week there were 2.85 pounds of jelly beans in a jar. By the end of the week, there were 1.7 pounds of jelly beans in the jar. Which is a more reasonable estimate for how many jelly beans were eaten during the week: 1 pound, 2 pounds, or 2.5 pounds?

   1 pound

5. In the morning, Kevin feeds his cat $\frac{1}{2}$ of a can of cat food, in the afternoon, the cat eats $\frac{1}{4}$ of a can of food, and in the evening, the cat eats $\frac{3}{4}$ of a can of food. Which is a more reasonable estimate for the amount of food the cat eats throughout the day: 1 can, 2 cans, or 3 cans?

   2 cans

6. A DVD player costs $154.98. A portable digital music player costs $174.49. Is $15, $20, or $25 a more reasonable estimate for how much more the digital music player costs?

   $20

Name _____ Date _____

10-5 Reteach

Problem-Solving Strategy: Determine Reasonable Answers

Linden buys $1\frac{3}{4}$ pounds of cashew nuts and $1\frac{1}{4}$ pounds of peanuts. He mixes the nuts together. About how many pounds of nuts are there altogether?

Step 1 Understand

What do you know?
• You know the amount of cashew nuts and the amount of peanuts.

What do you need to find?
You need to find about how many pounds of nuts there are altogether.

Step 2 Plan

You can use estimation to find a reasonable answer.

Step 3 Solve

Round each amount to the nearest whole number. Then add.

$1\frac{3}{4} \rightarrow 2 \qquad 1\frac{1}{4} \rightarrow 1$

Linden bought about $2 + 1$ or 3 pounds of nuts.

Step 4 Check

Is the answer reasonable?
Yes, because $1\frac{3}{4} + 1\frac{1}{4} = 3$.

Answers (Lesson 10–5)

10-5 Skills Practice

Name _____ Date _____

Problem-Solving Strategy: Determine Reasonable Answers

Solve. Determine which answer is reasonable.

1. Ms. Montoya makes $2\frac{3}{4}$ pounds of goat cheese in the morning. In the afternoon, she makes $1\frac{1}{4}$ pounds of goat cheese. Is 3 pounds, 4 pounds, or 5 pounds a more reasonable estimate for how much goat cheese Ms. Montoya makes in one day?

4 pounds

2. The Wilsons decide to churn butter for a family project. The boys in the family make 2.5 pounds of butter. The girls in the family make 4.7 pounds of butter. Which is a more reasonable estimate for how much more butter the girls made than the boys: 2 pounds, 3 pounds, or 4 pounds?

2 pounds

3. Clara picks 5.75 bushels of apples. Franz picks 3.25 bushels of apples. Is 2 bushels, 3 bushels, or 4 bushels a more reasonable estimate for how many more bushels Clara picked than Franz?

3 bushels

4. On Monday, Tina makes 4.7 pounds of raisins from grapes. On Tuesday, she makes 3.8 pounds of raisins. Which is a more reasonable estimate for about how many pounds of raisins she made in all: 7 pounds, 8 pounds, or 9 pounds?

9 pounds

5. Miguel picked 3.68 pounds of grapes last week. This week, he picks 2.27 pounds of grapes. Is 5 pounds, 6 pounds, or 7 pounds a more reasonable estimate for how many pounds Miguel picked altogether?

6 pounds

10-5 Homework Practice

Name _____ Date _____

Problem-Solving Strategy: Determine Reasonable Answers

Solve. Determine which answer is reasonable.

1. Marci found $1.42 in her coat pocket. She had $4.85 in her backpack. Is $5.50, $6.50, or $7.50 a more reasonable estimate for how much money she had altogether?

$6.50

2. James and a friend picked strawberries. James picked $4\frac{3}{5}$ pounds, and his friend picked $5\frac{4}{5}$ pounds. Which is a more reasonable estimate for how many pounds they picked altogether: 10 pounds, 11 pounds, or 12 pounds?

11 pounds

3. After school, Philipe spent $1\frac{3}{4}$ hour at baseball practice, $2\frac{1}{4}$ hour on homework, and $\frac{1}{4}$ hour getting ready for bed. Which is a more reasonable estimate for how long he spent on his activities: 3 hours, 4 hours, or 5 hours?

4 hours

4. Lynn went shopping at a local store. She bought 5 CDs, for $15.99 each, some candy for $1.79, and gloves for $5.89. Is $85, $88, or $90 a more reasonable estimate for how much money she spent altogether?

$88

Spiral Review

Subtract. Write each difference in simplest form. (Lesson 10–4)

5. $\frac{3}{6} - \frac{2}{12} = \frac{1}{3}$

6. $\frac{5}{5} - \frac{9}{15} = \frac{2}{5}$

7. $\frac{1}{2} - \frac{2}{8} = \frac{1}{4}$

8. $\frac{3}{4} - \frac{3}{8} = \frac{3}{8}$

9. $\frac{10}{12} - \frac{1}{2} = \frac{1}{3}$

10. $\frac{8}{9} - \frac{2}{3} = \frac{2}{9}$

11. $\frac{4}{5} - \frac{12}{20} = \frac{1}{5}$

12. $\frac{2}{3} - \frac{7}{15} = \frac{1}{5}$

Answers

10-5 Enrich

Name _____ Date _____

Enrich
Dr. Ken's Computer Cures

Use the data from the advertisement to solve the problems. Explain your answers.

> **—Dr. Ken's Computer Cures—**
>
> Repairs at Ken's: $49 per hour
> House calls: $75 flat fee, plus $79 per hour
> Web Site Design: $55 per hour
> Computer Tutoring: $40 per hour
> Network Design and Setup: $65 per hour
> Home Computer Setup: $200

1. On Monday, Dr. Ken's schedule lists 3 home computer setups and 4 hours of Web site design. Dr. Ken estimates that he will earn $1,000. Is his estimate reasonable?
   No: $3 \times \$200 = \$600$ and $4 \times 55 = \$220$. Since $\$600 + \$220 = \$820$, his estimate is not reasonable.

2. Dr. Ken makes a house call to Leah. He spends 3 hours fixing her computer. Leah estimates that her bill will be about $315. Is her estimate reasonable?
   Yes: $79 is to $80. $3 \times \$80 = \$240$, and $\$240 + \$75 = \$315$.

3. The Computer Whiz charges $46 per hour for Web site design. The Computer Whiz spends 22 hours designing a Web site for Regina. Regina estimates that she saved $400 by using The Computer Whiz instead of Dr. Ken. Is Regina's estimate reasonable?
   No; The Computer Whiz charges $9 less per hour than Dr. Ken. Since $\$10 + \$22 = \$220$, and estimate of $400 is not reasonable.

4. Dr. Ken tutors a group of 3 people for 4 hours. He charges a group rate of $32.50 per person per hour. Dr. Ken estimates that he earns $200 more than he would have if he had tutored just one person for the same amount of time at his regular rate. Is his estimate reasonable?
   Yes; since $3 \times \$30 = \$90$, and $4 \times \$90 = \$360$, Dr. Ken earns about $360 from the group. Dr. Ken would have earned $160 ($4 \times \$40$) by tutoring one person for 4 hours.

Grade 5   32   Chapter 10

10-6 Reteach

Name _____ Date _____

Reteach
Estimate Sums and Differences

You can round mixed numbers to the nearest whole number to estimate sums and differences of mixed numbers. Use number lines to help you.

Estimate $5\frac{5}{8} - 2\frac{1}{5}$

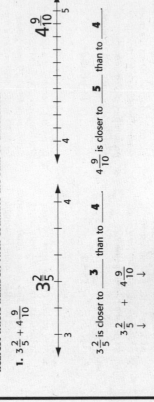

$5\frac{5}{8}$ is closer to 6 than to 5.
$5\frac{5}{8} \rightarrow$
$2\frac{1}{5}$ is closer to 2 than to 3.
$2\frac{1}{5} \rightarrow$
$6 - 2 = 4$ So, $5\frac{5}{8} - 2\frac{1}{5}$ is about 4.

Show each mixed number on a number line and round it to the nearest whole number. Then estimate the sum or difference.

1. $3\frac{2}{5} + 4\frac{9}{10}$

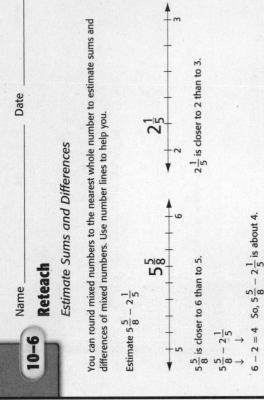

$3\frac{2}{5}$ is closer to __3__ than to __4__ $4\frac{9}{10}$ is closer to __5__ than to __4__

$3\frac{2}{5} \rightarrow$
$4\frac{9}{10} \rightarrow$

$\dfrac{3 + 5}{} = 8$

Estimate by rounding each mixed number to the nearest whole number.

2. $8\frac{9}{16} - 4\frac{1}{6} \rightarrow$ 3. $7\frac{9}{10} + 6\frac{7}{10} \rightarrow$ 4. $9\frac{7}{12} - 1\frac{3}{8} \rightarrow$

$\dfrac{9 - 5}{} = 4$ $\dfrac{8 + 7}{} = 15$ $\dfrac{10 - 1}{} = 9$

Grade 5   33   Chapter 10

Name _____ Date _____

10-6

Homework Practice
Estimate Sums and Differences

Estimate.

1. $4\frac{1}{3} + \frac{1}{8}$ $4 + 1 = 5$

2. $7\frac{1}{6} + \frac{8}{15}$ $7 + 1 = 8$

3. $\frac{9}{10} + 3\frac{2}{3}$ $1 + 4 = 5$

4. $8\frac{7}{8} - 1\frac{6}{9}$ $9 - 2 = 7$

5. $1\frac{2}{10} + 3\frac{1}{9}$ $1 + 3 = 4$

6. $7\frac{1}{3} + 7\frac{1}{8}$ $7 + 7 = 14$

7. $3\frac{5}{8} + 6\frac{3}{5}$ $4 + 7 = 11$

8. $\frac{8}{15} + 2\frac{5}{9}$ $1 + 3 = 4$

9. $6\frac{7}{8} - 4\frac{1}{7}$ $7 - 1 = 6$

10. $10\frac{7}{8} - \frac{5}{9}$ $11 - 1 = 10$

Spiral Review

Solve. Determine which answer is reasonable. (Lesson 10–5)

11. A store sells 12 pounds of apples. Of those, $5\frac{1}{2}$ pounds are green apples and $2\frac{1}{4}$ are golden. Which is a more reasonable estimate for how many more pounds of green apples than golden apples were sold: 3 pounds, 4 pounds, or 5 pounds?

3 pounds

12. Kelly has $92.63 in the bank. She wants a jacket for $91.00, but must keep at least $25 in the bank. Is $20, $25, or $30 a more reasonable estimate for how much more money she needs?

$25

Grade 5   35   Chapter 10

Answers

Name _____ Date _____

10-6

Skills Practice
Estimate Sums and Differences

Round each mixed number to the nearest whole number.

1. $7\frac{3}{4}$ **8**   2. $4\frac{1}{6}$ **4**   3. $8\frac{4}{10}$ **8**   4. $3\frac{4}{5}$ **4**

5. $2\frac{9}{16}$ **3**   6. $9\frac{4}{5}$ **10**   7. $1\frac{7}{8}$ **2**   8. $5\frac{5}{12}$ **5**

Estimate.

9. $3\frac{7}{8} + 2\frac{1}{6}$ $4 + 2 = 6$

10. $8\frac{5}{6} - 3\frac{2}{3}$ $9 - 4 = 5$

11. $5\frac{1}{8} - 1\frac{7}{8}$ $5 - 2 = 3$

12. $9\frac{7}{10} + 3\frac{4}{5}$ $10 + 4 = 14$

13. $6\frac{1}{4} + 7\frac{3}{8}$ $6 + 7 = 13$

14. $14\frac{1}{5} - 9\frac{3}{5}$ $14 - 10 = 4$

15. $18\frac{5}{16} - 9\frac{13}{16}$ $18 - 10 = 8$

16. $6\frac{11}{12} + 4\frac{5}{12}$ $7 + 4 = 11$

17. $7\frac{1}{3} + 7\frac{7}{12}$ $7 + 8 = 15$

18. $15\frac{3}{8} - 7\frac{7}{16}$ $15 - 7 = 8$

19. $9\frac{4}{5} + 6\frac{2}{3}$ $10 + 7 = 17$

20. $6\frac{11}{12} - 6\frac{1}{5}$ $7 - 6 = 1$

21. $8\frac{2}{5} + 8\frac{11}{16}$ $8 + 9 = 17$

22. $17\frac{7}{10} - 9\frac{1}{3}$ $18 - 9 = 9$

23. $7\frac{1}{3} + 9\frac{3}{8}$ $7 + 9 = 16$

24. $30\frac{7}{12} + 30\frac{1}{12}$ $31 + 30 = 61$

25. $58\frac{4}{5} - 29\frac{7}{8}$ $59 - 30 = 29$

26. $50\frac{5}{16} - 30\frac{1}{3}$ $50 - 30 = 20$

Solve.

27. Beth walks $10\frac{7}{8}$ miles in one week. She walks $2\frac{1}{4}$ fewer miles the following week. About how many miles does she walk the second week?
about 9 miles

28. Jon wants to walk at least 8 miles by the end of the week. He walks $5\frac{3}{4}$ miles by Thursday. If he walks another $2\frac{5}{8}$ miles on Friday, will he meet his goal? Explain.
yes, he walked about 9 miles

Grade 5   34   Chapter 10

10-6 Enrich

Name _____ Date _____

Estimate Sums and Differences

Round each mixed number to the nearest whole number. Then find three paths of four parts each. The estimated sums and differences of the mixed numbers on the paths must match the estimates at the finish lines. Do not use a number more than once.

Start
$6\frac{7}{8}$ mi
$+\frac{3}{16}$ mi
$-1\frac{7}{12}$
$+8\frac{5}{6}$ mi
About 20 mi
Finish

Start
$5\frac{1}{8}$ mi
$+5\frac{1}{3}$ mi
$20\frac{?}{?}$ mi
$+8\frac{?}{?}$ mi
About 8 mi
Finish

Start
$6\frac{?}{?}$ mi
$-2\frac{?}{?}$
$+7\frac{1}{8}$ mi
$+3\frac{?}{?}$ mi
About 4 mi
Finish

10-6 Problem-Solving Practice

Name _____ Date _____

Estimate Sums and Differences

Solve.

1. Abdul works $1\frac{3}{4}$ hour one day and $1\frac{1}{3}$ hour the next day. Estimate the total number of hours he works on both days combined.

   about ___**3**___ hours

2. Anna is making cookies for the school bake sale. If she uses $1\frac{1}{8}$ pounds of flour per batch, what is the amount of flour she needs for four batches?

   about ___**4**___ pounds

3. Rachel sings in a chorus at a concert. The songs are $4\frac{3}{10}$ minutes, $7\frac{1}{12}$ minutes, and $10\frac{3}{4}$ minutes long. Estimate the amount of time the chorus spends singing.

   about ___**22**___ minutes

4. Kathy rides her bicycle to her aunt's house. It takes her $20\frac{2}{3}$ minutes to get there. She is tired when she leaves, and it takes her $24\frac{1}{6}$ minutes to ride home. What is the approximate difference in the two times?

   about ___**3**___ minutes

5. Carol wants to make a picture frame for an 8×10 inch photo. The long pieces of the frame need to be $12\frac{1}{8}$ inches long. The short pieces should be $10\frac{1}{4}$ inches long. Estimate the length of wood Carol must buy to make the frame.

   about ___**44**___ inches

   Would this length be the actual amount she should buy? Explain.

   The estimate is an approximate length. Since all numbers were rounded down, she will need extra wood.

6. Justin plays football. On one play, he ran the ball $24\frac{1}{3}$ yards. The following play, he was tackled and lost $3\frac{2}{3}$ yards. The next play, he ran for $5\frac{1}{4}$ yards. Estimate how much farther the ball is down the field after the three plays.

   about ___**25**___ yards

Answers (Lesson 10–7)

10-7 Reteach

Add Mixed Numbers

Add $2\frac{4}{6} + 4\frac{3}{6}$

Step 1 Add the whole numbers.

$$2\frac{4}{6}$$
$$+\,4\frac{3}{6}$$
$$\overline{\phantom{2\frac{4}{6}}6}$$

Step 2 Add the fractions.

$$2\frac{4}{6}$$
$$+\,4\frac{3}{6}$$
$$\overline{6\frac{7}{6}}$$

Step 3 Simplify if possible.

$$6\frac{7}{6} = 7\frac{1}{6}$$

So, $2\frac{4}{6} + 4\frac{3}{6} = 7\frac{1}{6}$.

Add. Write each sum in simplest form.

1. $3\frac{5}{9} + 4\frac{2}{9} = 7\frac{7}{9}$

2. $4\frac{1}{15} + 5\frac{11}{15} = 9\frac{14}{15}$

3. $2\frac{1}{2} + 4 = 6\frac{1}{2}$

4. $8\frac{2}{5} + 4\frac{1}{10} = 12\frac{1}{2}$

5. $7\frac{6}{8} + 2\frac{1}{8} = 9\frac{7}{8}$

6. $2\frac{7}{10} + 3\frac{2}{10} = 5\frac{9}{10}$

7. $7\frac{2}{9} + 1\frac{4}{9} = 8\frac{2}{3}$

8. $8\frac{3}{14} + 2\frac{1}{7} = 10\frac{5}{14}$

9. $9\frac{3}{8} + 2\frac{1}{2} = 11\frac{7}{8}$

10. $1\frac{3}{4} + 4\frac{7}{8} = 6\frac{5}{8}$

11. $7\frac{4}{6} + 8\frac{5}{6} = 16\frac{1}{2}$

12. $1\frac{6}{15} + 9\frac{10}{15} = 11\frac{1}{15}$

13. $6\frac{3}{4} + 8\frac{4}{5} = 15\frac{11}{20}$

14. $3\frac{4}{6} + 5\frac{5}{6} = 9\frac{1}{2}$

15. $4\frac{4}{10} + 6\frac{7}{10} = 11\frac{1}{10}$

16. $8\frac{1}{16} + 4\frac{10}{16} = 12\frac{11}{16}$

17. $2\frac{6}{8} + 1\frac{5}{8} = 4\frac{3}{8}$

18. $8\frac{6}{9} + 1\frac{5}{9} = 10\frac{2}{9}$

19. $4\frac{12}{20} + 4\frac{15}{20} = 9\frac{7}{20}$

20. $5\frac{8}{12} + 2\frac{1}{4} = 7\frac{11}{12}$

10-7 Skills Practice

Add Mixed Numbers

Add. Write each sum in simplest form.

1. $5\frac{8}{12} + 3\frac{9}{12} = 9\frac{5}{12}$

2. $12\frac{7}{8} + 4\frac{2}{8} = 17\frac{1}{8}$

3. $13\frac{5}{10} + 4\frac{6}{10} = 18\frac{1}{10}$

4. $21\frac{8}{24} + 5\frac{7}{24} = 26\frac{5}{8}$

5. $8\frac{5}{10} + 6\frac{8}{10} = 15\frac{3}{10}$

6. $5\frac{9}{24} + 6\frac{22}{24} = 12\frac{7}{24}$

7. $5\frac{5}{15} + 2\frac{3}{15} = 7\frac{8}{15}$

8. $9\frac{4}{8} + 8\frac{4}{8} = 18$

9. $4\frac{2}{12} + 11\frac{6}{12} = 15\frac{2}{3}$

10. $7\frac{9}{15} + 1\frac{1}{5} = 8\frac{4}{5}$

11. $4\frac{3}{10} + 5\frac{4}{10} = 9\frac{7}{10}$

12. $3\frac{7}{8} + 2\frac{4}{8} = 6\frac{3}{8}$

13. $5\frac{2}{12} + 3\frac{3}{12} = 8\frac{5}{12}$

14. $6\frac{3}{4} + 2\frac{2}{4} = 9\frac{1}{4}$

15. $1\frac{1}{12} + 3\frac{2}{12} = 4\frac{1}{4}$

16. $9\frac{4}{10} + 10\frac{3}{10} = 19\frac{7}{10}$

17. $7\frac{4}{12} + 5\frac{11}{12} = 13\frac{1}{4}$

18. $11\frac{7}{10} + 4 = 15\frac{7}{10}$

19. $2\frac{8}{12} + 4\frac{9}{12} = 7\frac{5}{12}$

20. $7\frac{6}{8} + 2\frac{7}{8} = 10\frac{5}{8}$

21. $4\frac{3}{6} + 3\frac{5}{6} = 8\frac{1}{3}$

22. $7\frac{4}{6} + 1\frac{5}{6} = 9\frac{1}{2}$

23. $2\frac{1}{4} + 4\frac{15}{20} = 7$

24. $5\frac{3}{8} + 7\frac{4}{16} = 12\frac{5}{8}$

25. $14\frac{5}{16} + 8\frac{3}{8} = 22\frac{11}{16}$

26. $15\frac{6}{8} + 12\frac{10}{16} = 28\frac{3}{8}$

27. $9\frac{2}{12} + 4\frac{15}{18} = 14$

28. $12\frac{1}{3} + 6\frac{2}{6} = 18\frac{2}{3}$

Solve.

29. A cave is $5\frac{2}{4}$ miles west of a waterfall. A group of hikers is $2\frac{1}{4}$ miles east of the waterfall. How far is the group of hikers from the cave?

$7\frac{3}{4}$ miles

30. A mark on the side of a pier shows that the water is $4\frac{7}{8}$ ft deep. When the tide is high, the depth increases by $2\frac{3}{4}$ ft. What is the depth of the water when the tide is high?

$7\frac{5}{8}$ ft

Answers

Answers (Lesson 10–7)

Problem-Solving Practice

10–7

Name _____ Date _____

Problem-Solving Practice
Add Mixed Numbers

Add. Write each sum in simplest form.

1. Manuel walked $\frac{2}{3}$ of a mile to the park. He walked the same distance back home. How far did Manuel walk altogether?

   $1\frac{1}{3}$ miles

2. Blanca's children are $6\frac{1}{6}$ years old and $5\frac{2}{6}$ years old. In simplest form, what are the combined ages of her children?

   $11\frac{1}{2}$ years

3. Cumberland Valley Coal Company mines $249\frac{2}{3}$ tons of coal on one day and $387\frac{2}{6}$ tons on another day. What is the total number of tons of coal mined on both days?

   637 tons

4. Bethany bought $2\frac{1}{2}$ pounds of bread, $3\frac{1}{4}$ pounds of meat, and $3\frac{2}{8}$ pounds of cheese to make sandwiches for a party. She also bought $2\frac{1}{4}$ pounds of tomatoes, $1\frac{4}{16}$ pounds of onions, and $2\frac{3}{4}$ pounds of lettuce.
   What is the total number of pounds of food that she bought?

   $15\frac{1}{4}$ pounds

5. Keith is making a canvas tent. He needs $12\frac{3}{4}$ yards of beige canvas for the top and $8\frac{2}{4}$ yards of green canvas for the bottom. How many yards of canvas does he need in all?

   $21\frac{1}{4}$ yards

Homework Practice

10–7

Name _____ Date _____

Homework Practice
Add Mixed Numbers

Add. Write each sum in simplest form.

1. $7\frac{15}{16} - 2\frac{11}{16} =$ **$5\frac{1}{4}$**

2. $11\frac{8}{10} + 4\frac{3}{10} =$ **$16\frac{1}{10}$**

3. $12\frac{1}{3} + 9\frac{1}{3} =$ **$21\frac{2}{3}$**

4. $18\frac{1}{6} + 9\frac{5}{6} =$ **28**

5. $9\frac{2}{12} + 5\frac{1}{12} =$ **$14\frac{1}{4}$**

6. $16\frac{1}{3} + 7\frac{7}{10} =$ **$24\frac{1}{30}$**

7. $34\frac{11}{20} + 15\frac{1}{5} =$ **$49\frac{3}{4}$**

8. $64\frac{3}{4} + 37\frac{11}{12} =$ **$102\frac{2}{3}$**

9. $51\frac{1}{2} + 25\frac{3}{4} =$ **$77\frac{3}{20}$**

10. $46\frac{1}{4} + 27\frac{3}{4} =$ **74**

11. $82\frac{4}{5} + 62\frac{2}{5} =$ **$145\frac{1}{5}$**

12. $23\frac{1}{8} + 15\frac{2}{5} =$ **$38\frac{3}{5}$**

13. $16\frac{1}{4} + 7\frac{11}{12} =$ **$24\frac{1}{6}$**

14. $35\frac{7}{8} + 21\frac{4}{16} =$ **$57\frac{1}{8}$**

15. $97\frac{3}{5} + 87\frac{12}{15} =$ **$185\frac{2}{5}$**

16. $6\frac{11}{12}$
    $+ 4\frac{5}{12}$
    $11\frac{1}{3}$

17. $11\frac{2}{5}$
    $+ 3\frac{2}{5}$
    $14\frac{4}{5}$

18. $14\frac{14}{16}$
    $+ 5\frac{6}{8}$
    $20\frac{5}{8}$

19. $15\frac{1}{7}$
    $+ 6\frac{1}{4}$
    $21\frac{11}{28}$

Spiral Review

Estimate. (Lesson 10–6)

20. $\frac{4}{6} + 1\frac{5}{16} =$ **$1 + 2 = 3$**

21. $6\frac{9}{10} - 1\frac{2}{10} =$ **$7 - 1 = 6$**

22. $19\frac{1}{10} + 5\frac{9}{10} =$ **$19 + 6 = 25$**

23. $8\frac{11}{12} - 7\frac{1}{12} =$ **$9 - 7 = 2$**

10-8 Reteach

Name _____ Date _____

Subtract Mixed Numbers

Step 1 Subtract the fractions. Regroup if necessary.
Step 2 Subtract the whole numbers.
Step 3 Simplify if possible.

$$6\frac{2}{4} \rightarrow 5\frac{6}{4} \qquad 5\frac{6}{4} \qquad 5\frac{6}{4}$$
$$-2\frac{3}{4} \qquad\quad -2\frac{3}{4} \qquad -2\frac{3}{4}$$
$$\overline{\qquad\qquad} \qquad \overline{\frac{3}{4}} \qquad \overline{3\frac{3}{4}}$$

So, $6\frac{2}{4} - 2\frac{3}{4} = 3\frac{3}{4}$.
$3\frac{3}{4}$ is in simplest form.

Subtract. Write each difference in simplest form.

1. $7\frac{6}{8}$ $-3\frac{3}{8}$ = $\mathbf{4\frac{3}{8}}$
2. $2\frac{5}{16}$ $-1\frac{4}{16}$ = $\mathbf{1\frac{1}{16}}$
3. $9\frac{4}{5}$ $-4\frac{3}{5}$ = $\mathbf{5\frac{1}{5}}$
4. $21\frac{2}{16}$ $-11\frac{16}{16}$ = $\mathbf{10\frac{1}{6}}$
5. $15\frac{11}{12}$ $-11\frac{6}{12}$ = $\mathbf{4\frac{5}{12}}$

6. $12\frac{1}{4} - 4\frac{1}{8} =$ $\mathbf{8\frac{1}{8}}$
7. $3\frac{2}{3} - 1\frac{1}{6} =$ $\mathbf{2\frac{1}{2}}$
8. $6\frac{16}{20} - 2\frac{1}{4} =$ $\mathbf{4\frac{11}{20}}$
9. $41\frac{11}{12} - 27\frac{10}{12} =$ $\mathbf{14\frac{1}{12}}$
10. $70\frac{9}{10} - 45\frac{4}{5} =$ $\mathbf{25\frac{1}{10}}$
11. $10\frac{3}{5} - 3\frac{2}{5} =$ $\mathbf{7\frac{1}{5}}$
12. $3\frac{3}{8} - 1\frac{3}{4} =$ $\mathbf{1\frac{5}{8}}$
13. $4\frac{6}{12} - 1\frac{1}{2} =$ $\mathbf{3}$
14. $6\frac{3}{4} - 2\frac{3}{8} =$ $\mathbf{4\frac{1}{2}}$
15. $3\frac{3}{4} - 1\frac{3}{8} =$ $\mathbf{2\frac{1}{12}}$
16. $18\frac{3}{6} - 1\frac{1}{6} =$ $\mathbf{17\frac{1}{3}}$
17. $4\frac{3}{8} - 1\frac{1}{8} =$ $\mathbf{3\frac{1}{4}}$
18. $3\frac{3}{6} - 2\frac{1}{2} =$ $\mathbf{1}$
19. $4\frac{2}{3} - 1\frac{1}{3} =$ $\mathbf{3\frac{1}{3}}$
20. $25\frac{5}{8} - 17\frac{3}{8} =$ $\mathbf{8\frac{1}{4}}$

Grade 5 43 Chapter 10

10-7 Enrich

Name _____ Date _____

Add Mixed Numbers

Find the sums for the problems in the squares. Shade pairs of adjacent squares that have the same answer to find a path through the maze.

Start

$4\frac{7}{8}+3\frac{3}{8}$ $\mathbf{5\frac{1}{4}}$	$2\frac{1}{16}+3\frac{3}{16}$ $\mathbf{5\frac{1}{4}}$	$2\frac{7}{16}+5\frac{5}{16}$ $\mathbf{7\frac{3}{4}}$	$2\frac{7}{20}+1\frac{9}{20}$ $\mathbf{3\frac{4}{5}}$	$4\frac{1}{5}+1\frac{1}{5}$ $\mathbf{2\frac{3}{5}}$	$1\frac{8}{10}+8\frac{5}{10}$ $\mathbf{10\frac{3}{5}}$	$3\frac{1}{20}+1\frac{7}{20}$ $\mathbf{4\frac{2}{5}}$
$2\frac{5}{8}+2\frac{7}{8}$ $\mathbf{5\frac{1}{2}}$	$4\frac{7}{8}+2\frac{7}{8}$ $\mathbf{7\frac{3}{4}}$	$3\frac{5}{12}+2\frac{5}{12}$ $\mathbf{5\frac{3}{6}}$	$1\frac{11}{12}+1\frac{7}{12}$ $\mathbf{3\frac{5}{6}}$	$\frac{9}{10}+1\frac{7}{10}$ $\mathbf{2\frac{3}{5}}$	$\frac{9}{10}+\frac{9}{10}$ $\mathbf{1\frac{4}{5}}$	$2\frac{1}{2}+1\frac{1}{2}$ $\mathbf{4}$
$2\frac{1}{16}+1\frac{1}{8}$ $\mathbf{3\frac{3}{16}}$	$6\frac{5}{8}+1\frac{5}{8}$ $\mathbf{8\frac{1}{4}}$	$2\frac{5}{12}+2\frac{5}{12}$ $\mathbf{4\frac{5}{6}}$	$7\frac{1}{10}+2$ $\mathbf{9\frac{1}{10}}$	$3\frac{16}{20}+2\frac{5}{20}$ $\mathbf{6}$	$1\frac{13}{16}+2\frac{13}{16}$ $\mathbf{4\frac{5}{8}}$	$3\frac{7}{16}+1\frac{3}{16}$ $\mathbf{4\frac{5}{8}}$
$4\frac{1}{20}+2\frac{17}{20}$ $\mathbf{6\frac{9}{10}}$	$1\frac{7}{8}+7\frac{3}{8}$ $\mathbf{9\frac{1}{4}}$	$3\frac{1}{20}+2\frac{3}{20}$ $\mathbf{5\frac{1}{5}}$	$3\frac{3}{10}+1\frac{9}{10}$ $\mathbf{5\frac{1}{5}}$	$6\frac{4}{16}+7\frac{4}{16}$ $\mathbf{13\frac{1}{2}}$	$1\frac{3}{16}+1\frac{9}{16}$ $\mathbf{2\frac{3}{4}}$	$1\frac{5}{6}+\frac{5}{6}$ $\mathbf{2\frac{2}{3}}$
$3\frac{3}{9}+3\frac{1}{3}$ $\mathbf{6\frac{2}{3}}$	$8\frac{13}{16}+\frac{7}{16}$ $\mathbf{9\frac{1}{4}}$	$3\frac{3}{8}+1\frac{7}{8}$ $\mathbf{5\frac{1}{4}}$	$1\frac{14}{20}+1\frac{7}{10}$ $\mathbf{3\frac{2}{5}}$	$1\frac{3}{5}+2\frac{16}{20}$ $\mathbf{4\frac{2}{5}}$	$2\frac{7}{10}+1\frac{7}{10}$ $\mathbf{4\frac{2}{5}}$	$1\frac{7}{12}+1\frac{1}{12}$ $\mathbf{2\frac{2}{3}}$
$4\frac{14}{16}+1\frac{7}{8}$ $\mathbf{6\frac{3}{4}}$	$4\frac{9}{20}+2\frac{17}{20}$ $\mathbf{7\frac{3}{10}}$	$2\frac{18}{20}+5\frac{3}{10}$ $\mathbf{8\frac{1}{5}}$	$2\frac{4}{6}+3\frac{2}{3}$ $\mathbf{6\frac{1}{3}}$	$4\frac{1}{6}+2\frac{1}{6}$ $\mathbf{6\frac{1}{3}}$	$2\frac{5}{12}+2$ $\mathbf{4\frac{1}{2}}$	$1\frac{5}{6}+1\frac{5}{6}$ $\mathbf{3\frac{2}{3}}$
$4\frac{15}{16}+1\frac{13}{16}$ $\mathbf{5\frac{3}{4}}$	$2\frac{1}{16}+4\frac{11}{16}$ $\mathbf{6\frac{3}{4}}$	$5\frac{4}{5}+2\frac{8}{20}$ $\mathbf{8\frac{1}{5}}$	$3\frac{11}{12}+3\frac{11}{12}$ $\mathbf{7\frac{5}{6}}$	$3\frac{4}{6}+1\frac{2}{3}$ $\mathbf{5\frac{1}{3}}$	$2\frac{13}{16}+2\frac{9}{16}$ $\mathbf{5\frac{3}{8}}$	$3\frac{1}{16}+2\frac{5}{16}$ $\mathbf{5\frac{3}{8}}$

Finish

Grade 5 42 Chapter 10

Answers

10–8 Homework Practice
Subtract Mixed Numbers

Name _____ Date _____

Subtract. Write each difference in simplest form.

1. $2\frac{3}{4} - 1\frac{5}{8} = $ **$1\frac{1}{8}$**
2. $3\frac{2}{3} - 2\frac{1}{6} = $ **$1\frac{1}{2}$**
3. $3\frac{7}{12} - 1\frac{5}{12} = $ **$2\frac{1}{6}$**
4. $7\frac{3}{4} - 3\frac{7}{12} = $ **$4\frac{1}{6}$**
5. $5\frac{4}{9} - 2\frac{4}{9} = $ **$2\frac{1}{3}$**
6. $6\frac{3}{4} - 4\frac{1}{4} = $ **$2\frac{1}{2}$**
7. $3\frac{1}{2} - 1\frac{1}{2} = $ **2**
8. $4\frac{1}{2} - 2\frac{3}{8} = $ **$2\frac{1}{8}$**
9. $7\frac{1}{2} - 5\frac{4}{6} = $ **$1\frac{5}{6}$**
10. $12\frac{5}{8} - 4\frac{3}{8} = $ **$8\frac{1}{4}$**
11. $7\frac{9}{10} - 4\frac{1}{5} = $ **$7\frac{1}{10}$**
12. $13\frac{4}{5} - 4\frac{2}{5} = $ **$9\frac{2}{5}$**
13. $7\frac{20}{24} - 3\frac{6}{24} = $ **$4\frac{7}{12}$**
14. $12\frac{1}{2} - 4\frac{3}{10} = $ **$8\frac{1}{5}$**
15. $11\frac{3}{8} - 6\frac{1}{8} = $ **$5\frac{1}{4}$**
16. $14\frac{6}{10} - 6\frac{5}{10} = $ **$8\frac{1}{10}$**
17. $15\frac{3}{4} - 9\frac{2}{8} = $ **$6\frac{1}{2}$**
18. $17\frac{9}{10} - 8\frac{3}{10} = $ **$9\frac{3}{5}$**

Spiral Review
Add. Write each sum in simplest form. (Lesson 10–7)

19. $4\frac{3}{4} + 2\frac{3}{4} = $ **$7\frac{1}{2}$**
20. $5\frac{4}{9} + 4\frac{3}{9} = $ **$9\frac{7}{9}$**
21. $6\frac{5}{12} + 3\frac{1}{12} = $ **$9\frac{1}{2}$**
22. $8\frac{3}{7} + 5\frac{4}{7} = $ **14**

10–8 Skills Practice
Subtract Mixed Numbers

Name _____ Date _____

Subtract. Write each difference in simplest form.

1.
$$10\frac{11}{16} - 3\frac{14}{16} = \mathbf{6\frac{13}{16}}$$

2.
$$8\frac{5}{8} - 2\frac{3}{8} = \mathbf{6\frac{1}{4}}$$

3.
$$9\frac{3}{5} - 3\frac{2}{5} = \mathbf{6\frac{1}{5}}$$

4.
$$5\frac{6}{8} - 2\frac{4}{8} = \mathbf{3\frac{1}{2}}$$

5.
$$8\frac{3}{5} - 3\frac{2}{5} = \mathbf{5\frac{1}{5}}$$

6.
$$7\frac{1}{2} - 3\frac{3}{6} = \mathbf{4}$$

7.
$$2\frac{3}{4} - 1\frac{1}{8} = \mathbf{1\frac{5}{8}}$$

8.
$$4\frac{2}{16} - 2\frac{1}{16} = \mathbf{2\frac{1}{16}}$$

9.
$$9\frac{2}{3} - 3\frac{1}{3} = \mathbf{6\frac{1}{3}}$$

10.
$$2\frac{4}{5} - 1\frac{2}{5} = \mathbf{1\frac{2}{5}}$$

11. $15\frac{7}{12} - 8\frac{1}{2} = $ **$7\frac{1}{12}$**
12. $6\frac{7}{8} - 2\frac{7}{8} = $ **4**
13. $27\frac{7}{12} - 13\frac{1}{12} = $ **$14\frac{1}{2}$**
14. $5\frac{8}{20} - 1\frac{1}{4} = $ **$4\frac{3}{20}$**
15. $10\frac{2}{3} - 7\frac{1}{3} = $ **$3\frac{1}{3}$**
16. $7\frac{1}{3} - 2\frac{1}{9} = $ **$5\frac{2}{9}$**
17. $8\frac{3}{5} - 1\frac{2}{5} = $ **$7\frac{1}{5}$**
18. $10\frac{9}{10} - 2\frac{1}{5} = $ **$8\frac{7}{10}$**
19. $12\frac{3}{10} - 6\frac{1}{10} = $ **$6\frac{1}{5}$**
20. $5\frac{9}{12} - 3\frac{9}{12} = $ **2**
21. $15\frac{5}{8} - 7\frac{1}{8} = $ **$8\frac{1}{2}$**
22. $11\frac{6}{8} - 6\frac{5}{8} = $ **$5\frac{1}{8}$**

Solve.

23. Anna has $3\frac{1}{2}$ yd of fabric. She plans to use $2\frac{1}{4}$ yd for curtains. Does she have enough left to make 2 pillows that each use $1\frac{1}{4}$ yd of fabric? Explain.

no; she will have $1\frac{1}{4}$ yd left, which is not enough

24. Paula has 2 yd of elastic. One project needs a $\frac{3}{4}$-yd piece. Does she have enough for another project that needs $1\frac{1}{3}$ yd? Explain.

No; she will have only $1\frac{1}{4}$ yd left; $1\frac{1}{4} < 1\frac{1}{3}$

10-8 Problem Solving Practice

Name _____ Date _____

Subtract Mixed Numbers

Subtract. Write each difference in simplest form.

1. A large table is $30\frac{7}{16}$ inches high. A small table is $16\frac{5}{16}$ inches high. How much higher is the larger table?

   $14\frac{1}{8}$ in.

2. Brenda is $59\frac{3}{4}$ inches tall. Her sister is $48\frac{2}{8}$ inches tall. How much taller is Brenda than her sister?

   $11\frac{1}{2}$ in.

3. Wilma pitches $4\frac{2}{3}$ innings in a baseball game. Nina pitches $1\frac{2}{6}$ innings in the same game. How many more innings does Wilma pitch than Nina?

   $3\frac{1}{3}$ innings

4. Robert lives $3\frac{3}{10}$ miles from school. Al lives $4\frac{7}{10}$ miles from school. Who lives farther from school? How much farther?

   Al lives farther; $1\frac{2}{5}$ mi

5. Jayne needs $\frac{14}{16}$ of a yard of ribbon to decorate a banner. She has $\frac{5}{8}$ of a yard of ribbon. How much more ribbon does Jayne need?

   $\frac{1}{4}$ yd

6. Rick has a choice of buying $4\frac{3}{5}$ packages of pencils or $2\frac{2}{5}$ packages of pens. In simplest form, how many more packages of pencils than pens can he buy?

   $2\frac{1}{5}$ packages

7. One year, Cumberland Valley Coal Company planted $14\frac{3}{6}$ dozen trees to help prevent erosion. The following year, they planted $20\frac{3}{6}$ dozen trees. How many more trees did they plant the second year?

   $6\frac{1}{6}$ dozen

10-8 Enrich

Name _____ Date _____

Subtract Mixed Numbers

Play this game with a partner. You will need a counter.

- Together choose a whole number from 5 through 10. Write it in the square at the bottom right of the game board. Place your counter on Start. Then move it one square in any direction. Find the sum or difference of the numbers in the starting square and the square you moved to. If fractions don't have like denominators, try using an equivalent fraction to find the sum or difference. Record it on a separate sheet of paper.
- Players alternate turns. On each turn, move one square. Add or subtract the number in that square to or from your previous sum or difference and record your answer. You cannot return to a square.
- The winner is the first player who reaches the target square with a sum or difference equal to the target number.

				$1\frac{1}{3}$
			$4\frac{1}{2}$	
		$2\frac{1}{8}$		$2\frac{1}{4}$
		$1\frac{1}{4}$	$1\frac{4}{5}$	
		$1\frac{7}{10}$		$2\frac{5}{6}$
		$3\frac{1}{2}$	$1\frac{1}{2}$	
	$2\frac{2}{3}$			$3\frac{3}{8}$
		$\frac{5}{8}$	$\frac{3}{5}$	
	$\frac{1}{4}$			$\frac{3}{4}$
		$\frac{1}{5}$	$\frac{1}{2}$	
	$\frac{1}{8}$			
		$\frac{1}{6}$	$\frac{1}{3}$	Target Number _____

Start	$2\frac{1}{2}$	$1\frac{1}{6}$	$3\frac{5}{8}$
	$3\frac{1}{4}$	$2\frac{2}{5}$	$1\frac{2}{3}$
	$3\frac{2}{3}$	$1\frac{7}{8}$	$3\frac{1}{2}$
	$1\frac{3}{4}$	$1\frac{3}{8}$	$2\frac{2}{3}$
	$1\frac{1}{2}$	$2\frac{3}{10}$	$1\frac{1}{4}$
	$5\frac{1}{4}$	$2\frac{3}{4}$	$1\frac{1}{8}$

Name _____ Date _____

10-9

Reteach

Problem-Solving Strategy (continued)

Step 4
Check   **Is the solution reasonable?**

Look back at the problem.

Have you answered the question? _____ **yes**

Does your answer make sense? _____ **yes**

Did you find a pattern and continue it? _____ **yes**

Use any strategy to solve each problem.

1. On the first day of the crafts fair, 200 people show up. Each day after that, the number of people who attend the fair increases by 150. The craft fair runs for five days. How many people attend the fair on the last day?

   800 people

2. Find the next three numbers in the pattern below. Then describe the pattern.

   −5, 0, 5, 10, ___, ___, ___

   15, 20, 25; the pattern

   increases by 5s

3. Jamal, Diego, and Megan went shopping together and each bought a different type of clothing: a hat, a shirt, and a pair of shoes. Jamal did not buy something to put on his feet. Diego bought his item before the person bought the shoes. Either Megan or Diego bought the hat. What item did each person buy?

   Jamal: shirt; Diego: hat;

   Megan: shoes

4. A yellow, a green, and a blue marble are placed in a bag. If you take one marble out of the bag at a time, in how many different orders can all three marbles be removed from the bag? List all possibilities.

   6 orders; YGB, YBG, GYB,

   GBY, BYG, BGY

5. Mrs. Reynolds is buying sandwiches for the 10 students in her class as a reward. If she bought at least one of each type of sandwich and spent a total of $34.00, how many of each sandwich did she buy?

Sandwiches	
Type	**Price**
Italian	$4.00
Roast Beef	$3.50
Veggie	$3.00

   Sample answer: 3 Italian, 2 roast beef,

   and 5 veggie.

Grade 5   49   *Chapter 10*

Name _____ Date _____

10-9

Reteach

Problem-Solving Investigation: Choose the Best Strategy

Look for a Pattern

Gregory is practicing the high jump. If he starts the bar at 3 feet 4 inches and raises it 0.5 inch after each jump, how high will the bar be on the sixth jump?

Step 1
Understand   **What facts do you know?**

• Gregory starts the bar at   **3 feet 4 inches**

• Gregory raises the bar   **0.5 inch**   after each jump.

What do you need to find?   **the bar will be on the**

• You need to find how high   **sixth jump.**

Step 2
Plan   **Make a plan.**

Using a pattern will help you solve the problem.

Organize the information in a chart.

Step 3
Solve   **Carry out your plan.**

Make a chart. Look for a pattern in the chart.

Jump Number	1	2	3	4	5	6
Bar Height	3 feet 4 inches	3 feet 4.5 inches	3 feet 5 inches	3 feet 5.5 inches	3 feet 6 inches	**3 feet 6.5 inches**

Look at the chart to find the pattern.

What is the pattern?

Each jump increases by 0.5 inch.

Continue the pattern to predict the height for the sixth jump.

Jump 6: 3 feet 6 inches + 0.5 inch =   **3 feet 6.5 inches**

Using the pattern, you can expect that the bar will be set at

3 feet 6.5 inches   for the sixth jump.

Grade 5   48   *Chapter 10*

10–9

Homework Practice

Problem-Solving Investigation: Choose the Best Strategy

Use any strategy to solve each problem.

1. Describe the pattern below. Then, find the missing number.
50, 500, _____, 50,000.
The numbers are each multiplied by 10; 5,000

2. Melinda's mother is four times as old as Melinda. In 16 years, her mother will be twice her age. How old is Melinda now?
8 years old

3. Ginny has a piece of fabric 20 yards long. How many cuts will she make if she cuts the fabric into sections that are 2 yards long?
9 cuts

Spiral Review

Solve. Write each answer in simplest form. (Lesson 10–8)

4. Mr. Hernandez bought $12\frac{3}{4}$ gallons of paint to paint his house. He used $10\frac{1}{4}$ gallons. How much paint was left?
$2\frac{1}{2}$ gal

5. The length of Dawn's yard is $8\frac{4}{5}$ feet. Find the width of her yard if it is $1\frac{3}{5}$ feet shorter than the length.
$7\frac{1}{5}$ ft

6. Find eight and nine tenths minus three and four tenths. Write your answer in words.
five and one half

10–9

Skills Practice

Problem-Solving Investigation: Choose the Best Strategy

Use any strategy to solve each problem.

1. Describe the pattern below. Then find the missing number.
10, 20, 30, _____, 50
10 is added to each number; 40

2. Fifty five families that own pets were asked what type of pets they own. Of the families surveyed, 24 have dogs, 14 have cats, and 5 have both dogs and cats. How many have neither a dog nor cat?
22 families

3. A designer is making a tile mosaic. The first row of the mosaic has 1 red tile in the center. If the designer increases the number of red tiles in the center of each row by 4, how many red tiles will be in the center of the fifth row?
17 red tiles

4. Six students are sitting at a lunch table. Two more students arrive, and at the same time, three students leave. Then, four students leave, and two more arrive. How many students are at the table now?
3 students

5. The sum of two whole numbers between 20 and 40 is 58. The difference of the two numbers is 12. What are the two numbers?
35, 23

6. Ramon has $3.50. He buys two pens that cost $0.75 each and a pencil that costs $0.40. How much money does Ramon have left?
$1.60

Answers (Lessons 10–9 and 10–10)

10-10 Reteach

Name _____ Date _____

Subtraction with Renaming

Sometimes you need to rename fractions in order to subtract them.

Subtract $6\frac{2}{4} - 2\frac{3}{4}$.

Step 1 Regroup $6\frac{2}{4}$ as $5\frac{6}{4}$.	Step 2 Subtract the fractions.
$6\frac{2}{4} \rightarrow 5\frac{6}{4}$ $-2\frac{3}{4} \rightarrow -2\frac{3}{4}$	$5\frac{6}{4}$ $-2\frac{3}{4}$ $\frac{3}{4}$
Step 3 Subtract the whole numbers.	Step 4 Simplify if possible.
$5\frac{6}{4}$ $-2\frac{3}{4}$ $3\frac{3}{4}$	$3\frac{3}{4}$ is in simplest form.

So, $6\frac{1}{2} - 2\frac{3}{4} = 3\frac{3}{4}$.

Subtract. Write each difference in simplest form.

1. $7\frac{3}{8}$ $-3\frac{5}{8}$ = $3\frac{3}{4}$
2. $2\frac{3}{16}$ $-1\frac{9}{16}$ = $\frac{5}{8}$
3. $9\frac{2}{5}$ $-4\frac{4}{5}$ = $4\frac{3}{5}$
4. $21\frac{7}{12}$ $-11\frac{5}{6}$ = $9\frac{3}{4}$
5. $15\frac{1}{4}$ $-11\frac{3}{4}$ = $3\frac{1}{2}$

6. $12\frac{1}{4} - 4\frac{6}{8} = 7\frac{1}{2}$
7. $3\frac{1}{6} - 1\frac{4}{6} = 1\frac{1}{2}$
8. $6\frac{1}{5} - 2\frac{4}{5} = 3\frac{2}{5}$

9. $41\frac{2}{3} - 27\frac{11}{12} = 13\frac{3}{4}$
10. $70\frac{4}{10} - 45\frac{3}{5} = 24\frac{4}{5}$
11. $10\frac{4}{9} - 3\frac{7}{9} = 6\frac{2}{3}$

12. $3\frac{2}{8} - 1\frac{7}{8} = 1\frac{3}{8}$
13. $4\frac{5}{12} - 1\frac{3}{4} = 2\frac{2}{3}$
14. $6\frac{3}{5} - 2\frac{4}{5} = 3\frac{4}{5}$

15. $3\frac{10}{16} - 1\frac{7}{8} = 1\frac{3}{4}$
16. $18\frac{1}{3} - 13\frac{2}{3} = 4\frac{2}{3}$
17. $4\frac{3}{8} - 1\frac{7}{8} = 2\frac{1}{2}$

Grade 5   53   Chapter 10

10-9 Enrich

Name _____ Date _____

Multi-step Problems

Solve.

1. The outer edge of a picture frame forms a square. The square picture frame has sides of 18 inches. The width of the frame is 1 inch. What is the area of the picture within the frame? Remember, area is found by multiplying length times width.

256 square inches

2. Sammy has a $42\frac{1}{2}$ inch-long board. He cuts three $6\frac{1}{2}$ inch long pieces of wood from the board. Does Sammy have enough wood left to make a 24 inch long shelf? Explain.

No; he only has 23 inches of wood left

3. Theresa made a stack of cubes. Three of the cubes were $\frac{1}{2}$ inch on each side. Three of the cubes were $1\frac{1}{2}$ inches on each side. After Theresa removed a cube, the height of the stack was $4\frac{1}{2}$ inches. Which kind of cube did Theresa remove?

$1\frac{1}{2}$ inch cube

4. Mark was paid $10,000 to do some carpentry. He spent half of that money on suppplies and $1,000 to pay a helper. How much money did Mark earn for himself?

$4,000

Grade 5   52   Chapter 10

Copyright © Macmillan/McGraw-Hill, a division of The McGraw-Hill Companies, Inc.

Grade 5   A24   Chapter 10

Answers (Lesson 10–10)

10-10 Skills Practice

Subtraction with Renaming

Subtract. Write each difference in simplest form.

1. $10\frac{6}{16}$ − $3\frac{11}{16}$ = $6\frac{11}{16}$

2. $8\frac{1}{3}$ − $2\frac{2}{3}$ = $5\frac{2}{3}$

3. $9\frac{2}{5}$ − $3\frac{4}{5}$ = $5\frac{3}{5}$

4. $5\frac{3}{16}$ − $2\frac{1}{2}$ = $2\frac{11}{16}$

5. $8\frac{1}{6}$ − $3\frac{4}{6}$ = $4\frac{2}{3}$

6. $7\frac{5}{9}$ − $3\frac{8}{9}$ = $3\frac{2}{3}$

7. $2\frac{4}{4}$ − $1\frac{3}{4}$ = $1\frac{1}{2}$

8. $4\frac{4}{4}$ − $2\frac{5}{8}$ = $1\frac{5}{8}$

9. $5\frac{2}{5}$ − $1\frac{4}{5}$ = $3\frac{3}{5}$

10. $10\frac{1}{3}$ − $7\frac{2}{3}$ = $2\frac{2}{3}$

11. $7\frac{1}{4}$ − $2\frac{3}{4}$ = $4\frac{1}{2}$

12. $8\frac{2}{6}$ − $1\frac{5}{6}$ = $6\frac{1}{2}$

13. $10\frac{1}{3}$ − $2\frac{5}{9}$ = $7\frac{7}{9}$

14. $12\frac{2}{7}$ − $6\frac{6}{7}$ = $5\frac{3}{7}$

15. $5\frac{7}{12}$ − $3\frac{5}{6}$ = $1\frac{3}{4}$

16. $15\frac{1}{8}$ − $7\frac{5}{8}$ = $7\frac{1}{2}$

17. $11\frac{1}{4}$ − $6\frac{1}{2}$ = $4\frac{3}{4}$

Find each missing number.

18. $6\frac{2}{5}$ − $4\frac{\boxed{4}}{\boxed{5}}$ = $1\frac{3}{5}$

19. $15\frac{3}{12}$ + $8\frac{\boxed{7}}{\boxed{12}}$ = $6\frac{8}{12}$

20. $10\frac{1}{3}$ − $6\frac{\boxed{2}}{\boxed{3}}$ = $3\frac{2}{3}$

21. $6\frac{5}{9}$ − $2\frac{\boxed{8}}{\boxed{9}}$ = $3\frac{6}{9}$

Solve.

22. Anna has $3\frac{1}{4}$ yd of fabric. She uses $2\frac{3}{4}$ yd for curtains. How much fabric is left over?

$\frac{1}{2}$ yd

23. Paula has $2\frac{3}{6}$ yard of elastic. One project needs a $1\frac{4}{6}$ yard piece. Will she have enough elastic to make another project that uses the same amount? Explain.

No; she will have only $\frac{5}{6}$ yd left; $\frac{5}{6} < 1\frac{4}{6}$

10-10 Homework Practice

Subtraction with Renaming

Subtract. Write each difference in simplest form.

1. $7\frac{1}{4}$ − $4\frac{3}{4}$ = $2\frac{1}{2}$

2. $9\frac{2}{5}$ − $5\frac{3}{5}$ = $3\frac{4}{5}$

3. $6\frac{1}{3}$ − $2\frac{2}{3}$ = $3\frac{2}{3}$

4. $14\frac{1}{2}$ − $5\frac{1}{4}$ = $9\frac{1}{4}$

5. $10\frac{5}{8}$ − $6\frac{6}{8}$ = $3\frac{7}{8}$

6. $12\frac{1}{5}$ − $6\frac{8}{10}$ = $5\frac{2}{5}$

7. $5\frac{1}{2}$ − $4\frac{5}{6}$ = $\frac{2}{3}$

8. $3\frac{1}{3}$ − $1\frac{2}{3}$ = $1\frac{2}{3}$

9. $9\frac{4}{7}$ − $2\frac{6}{7}$ = $5\frac{5}{7}$

10. $3\frac{1}{4}$ − $1\frac{5}{8}$ = $1\frac{5}{8}$

11. $9\frac{8}{12}$ − $3\frac{11}{12}$ = $5\frac{3}{4}$

12. $2\frac{1}{10}$ − $1\frac{2}{5}$ = $\frac{7}{10}$

13. $15\frac{5}{9}$ − $8\frac{7}{9}$ = $6\frac{7}{9}$

14. $6\frac{7}{16}$ − $2\frac{6}{8}$ = $3\frac{11}{16}$

Spiral Review

Use any strategy to solve each problem. (Lesson 10-9)

- Make a graph.
- Determine reasonable answers.
- Act it out.
- Look for a pattern.

15. At a grocery store a bag of apples costs $1.79. A jar of jelly costs $0.25 less than a bag of apples. Find the total cost of these two items.

$3.33

16. A runner starts running 10 miles per week and adds $\frac{1}{2}$ mile each week. How far will she run in the seventh week?

13 miles

Answers

10–10 Problem-Solving Practice
Subtracting Mixed Numbers with Renaming

Name _____ Date _____

Solve.

1. When Shane and his family went on vacation, the pilot announced that it would take $4\frac{1}{4}$ hours to reach their destination. When the flight snack was served, they had been in flight $2\frac{3}{4}$ hours. How much longer was the flight after the snack was served?

   $1\frac{1}{2}$ hours

2. Mark bought $5\frac{1}{4}$ pounds of yellow cheese and $3\frac{3}{4}$ of white cheese. How much more yellow cheese than white cheese did he buy?

   $1\frac{1}{2}$ pounds

3. Stella made $4\frac{5}{8}$ quarts of lemon tea for the weekend barbecue. Vincent made $2\frac{7}{8}$ quarts of mint tea for the barbecue. How much more tea did Stella make than Vincent?

   $1\frac{3}{4}$ quarts

4. Taylor's puppy weighs $9\frac{2}{10}$ pounds. Belinda's kitten weighs $3\frac{3}{5}$ pounds. How much more does Taylor's puppy weigh than Belinda's kitten?

   $5\frac{3}{5}$ pounds

5. Jillian has a piece of leather cord that is $12\frac{1}{5}$ inches long. She only needs $8\frac{4}{5}$ inches of cord to make a bracelet. How much leather cord will she trim?

   $3\frac{2}{5}$ inches

10–10 Enrich
More Mixed Numbers

Name _____ Date _____

Find a path through the maze. Shade the spaces that connect two equivalent numbers. (*Hint:* Rename fractions if you get stuck!)

$3\frac{2}{5}$	$2\frac{7}{5}$	$2\frac{3}{5}$	$3\frac{3}{10}$	$\frac{18}{5}$	$3\frac{3}{5}$	$\frac{36}{5}$
$3\frac{5}{9}$	$3\frac{3}{4}$	$\frac{12}{4}$	$6\frac{1}{2}$	$\frac{11}{2}$	$2\frac{7}{10}$	$\frac{27}{100}$
$4\frac{1}{4}$	$\frac{15}{4}$	$3\frac{1}{4}$	$7\frac{1}{2}$	$\frac{13}{2}$	$\frac{27}{5}$	$\frac{27}{10}$
$4\frac{19}{20}$	$\frac{119}{25}$	$\frac{44}{25}$	$\frac{5}{4}$	$\frac{7}{4}$	$5\frac{1}{2}$	$5\frac{1}{5}$
$3\frac{3}{4}$	$4\frac{19}{25}$	$6\frac{1}{3}$	$1\frac{1}{4}$	$1\frac{1}{5}$	$\frac{11}{2}$	$10\frac{1}{2}$
$\frac{19}{4}$	$4\frac{1}{4}$	$\frac{20}{3}$	$\frac{15}{3}$	$2\frac{11}{20}$	$\frac{51}{20}$	$2\frac{5}{11}$
$4\frac{1}{2}$	$4\frac{3}{4}$	$\frac{3}{4}$	$6\frac{2}{3}$	$6\frac{1}{4}$	$\frac{10}{53}$	$5\frac{3}{10}$
$\frac{19}{8}$	$2\frac{5}{8}$	$\frac{23}{8}$	$\frac{29}{20}$	$1\frac{4}{5}$	$\frac{53}{10}$	$3\frac{3}{10}$
$3\frac{3}{8}$	$2\frac{7}{8}$	$\frac{21}{8}$	$1\frac{9}{20}$	$1\frac{5}{16}$	$\frac{18}{5}$	$3\frac{3}{5}$

Answers (Vocabulary Test and Oral Assessment)

---

10 **Vocabulary Test**

Name _____ Date _____

Match each word to its definition. Write your answers on the lines provided.

1. like fractions **C**	A. the form of a fraction when the GCF of the numerator and the denominator is one
2. simplest form **A**	B. a number in which the numerator is greater than the denominator
3. denominator **E**	C. fractions that have the same denominator
4. improper fraction **B**	D. the part of the fraction that tells how many of the equal parts are being used
5. numerator **D**	E. the bottom number in a fraction
6. unlike fractions **F**	F. fractions that have a different denominator

Assessment

---

10 **Oral Assessment**

Student Name _____ Date _____

Use construction paper to cut out the following 3 labeled shapes:

1	
$\frac{1}{2}$	$\frac{1}{2}$

$\frac{1}{4}$	$\frac{1}{4}$	$\frac{1}{4}$
$\frac{1}{4}$		

Read each question aloud to the student. Then write the student's answers on the lines below the questions.

1. How are these shapes labeled?
   One is labeled 1, another is labeled $\frac{1}{2}$ and $\frac{1}{2}$, and the third is labeled with four sections that all say $\frac{1}{4}$.

2. Let's line these shapes up against each other. Are all the shapes the same length?
   Yes

3. Let's look at the shape labeled 1 and the shape labeled $\frac{1}{2}$ and $\frac{1}{2}$. Let's put them next to each other. What do you notice?
   Answers may vary. Student may say that one of the shapes is divided into halves or into 2 sections

4. Look at the shape labeled $\frac{1}{2}$ and $\frac{1}{2}$. Think of a sentence you can tell me about what $\frac{1}{2}$ and $\frac{1}{2}$ equal.
   Answers may vary. Student may say that $\frac{1}{2} + \frac{1}{2} = 1$.

5. Hold the shape labeled 1 next to the shape with labeled $\frac{1}{2}$ and $\frac{1}{2}$. Is your sentence correct? How do you know?
   Answers will vary. Student may say that the two shapes are the same size, so $\frac{1}{2} + \frac{1}{2} = 1$.

Answers

Answers (Oral Assessment)

10

Student Name _____ Date _____

Oral Assessment   (continued)

6. Now let's look at the shape labeled with the $\frac{1}{4}$s. How is it different from the first two shapes?

   Answers may vary. Student may say

   that it has more sections in it.

7. How many sections are there in this shape?

   4

8. Tell how you got your answer.

   Student may say, "I counted the sections."

9. Let's look at the shape labeled with the $\frac{1}{4}$s next to the shape labeled 1. Are these shapes the same length?

   Yes

10. How many $\frac{1}{4}$s are there in every shape labeled 1?

    4

11. How do you know?

    Answers may vary. Student may say, "I counted them."

12. Tell a number sentence about the shape with the $\frac{1}{4}$s.

    $$\frac{1}{4} + \frac{1}{4} + \frac{1}{4} + \frac{1}{4} = 1$$

13. Let's look at the shape labeled $\frac{1}{2} + \frac{1}{2}$ next to the shape labeled $\frac{1}{4} + \frac{1}{4} + \frac{1}{4} + \frac{1}{4}$. Tell how these shapes are related.

    Answers may vary. Student may say,

    "$\frac{1}{2} + \frac{1}{2}$ is the same as $\frac{1}{4} + \frac{1}{4} + \frac{1}{4} + \frac{1}{4}$."

14. How do you know?

    Student may say, "I can see that they are the same."

15. Can you think of a time when you used fractions?

    Answers will vary.

Assessment

Chapter 10 Assessment Answer Key

Chapter Diagnostic Test Page 59	Chapter Pretest Page 60	Quiz 1 Page 61
1. $\dfrac{1}{2}$	1. $\dfrac{4}{5}$	1. $\dfrac{6}{7}$
2. $\dfrac{1}{4}$	2. $1\dfrac{2}{9}$	2. $\dfrac{8}{9}$
3. $\dfrac{3}{5}$	3. $>$	3. $\dfrac{5}{9}$
4. $\dfrac{1}{6}$		4. $\dfrac{1}{7}$
5. $\dfrac{1}{3}$	4. $\$8.65$	5. $1\dfrac{4}{}$
6. $1\dfrac{4}{5}$	5. No	6. $\dfrac{5}{8}$
7. $1\dfrac{1}{3}$		7. two ninths
8. $1\dfrac{5}{7}$		
9. $4\dfrac{1}{6}$	6. 7	8. 50
10. $1\dfrac{1}{2}$	7. $8\dfrac{3}{8}$	9. 8 pounds
11. 4	8. $13\dfrac{5}{9}$	10. $\$3$
12. 8	9. $\dfrac{3}{4}$	
13. 7	10. $11\dfrac{1}{4}$	
14. 8		
15. about $\$10$		

Answers

Chapter 10 Assessment Answer Key

Quiz 2
Page 62

1. $5 + 1 = 6$
2. $2 + 7 = 9$
3. $1 + 1 = 2$
4. $6\frac{2}{5}$
5. 6
6. $2\frac{3}{4}$
7. 12 pounds
8. $4\frac{1}{10}$
9. $5\frac{2}{3}$
10. $11\frac{1}{3}$

Quiz 3
Page 63

1. $12.87
2. 49 inches
3. $1\frac{1}{2}$ feet
4. 2 quarters, 2 dimes, 1 nickel, and 2 pennies
5. $\frac{3}{4}$
6. $2\frac{3}{5}$
7. $2\frac{4}{9}$
8. $4\frac{5}{6}$
9. $8\frac{7}{9}$

Mid-Chapter Review
Page 64

1. $\frac{5}{6}$
2. $\frac{2}{3}$
3. 1
4. $12.11
5. 44.5 inches
6. $1\frac{1}{2}$ feet
7. $2 - 2 = 0$
8. $6 - 2 = 4$
9. $3 + 2 = 5$
10. $10 + 5 = 15$

Chapter 10 Assessment Answer Key

Chapter Test, Form 1
Page 70

1. __B__
2. __G__
3. __C__
4. __H__
5. __C__
6. __H__
7. __B__

Page 71

8. __G__
9. __B__
10. __G__
11. __B__
12. __H__
13. __C__
14. __J__

Chapter Test, Form 2A
Page 72

1. __B__
2. __H__
3. __B__
4. __J__
5. __B__
6. __F__
7. __B__

(continued on the next page)

Copyright © Macmillan/McGraw-Hill, a division of The McGraw-Hill Companies, Inc.

Chapter 10 Assessment Answer Key

**Chapter Test,
Form 2A** *(continued)*
Page 73

Chapter Test, Form 2B

Page 74

Page 75

8. **G**

9. **A**

10. **F**

11. **C**

12. **H**

13. **A**

14. **J**

1. **B**

2. **F**

3. **C**

4. **J**

5. **A**

6. **F**

7. **A**

8. **H**

9. **A**

10. **J**

11. **B**

12. **H**

13. **B**

14. **F**

Chapter 10 Assessment Answer Key

Chapter Test, Form 2C
Page 76

1. __B__

2. __G__

3. __C__

4. __H__

5. __A__

6. __F__

7. __B__

Page 77

8. __F__

9. __B__

10. __F__

11. __B__

12. __J__

13. __B__

14. __H__

Chapter Test, Form 2D
Page 78

1. __B__

2. __G__

3. __A__

4. __H__

5. __B__

6. __H__

7. __D__

(continued on the next page)

Answers

Chapter 10 Assessment Answer Key

Chapter Test, Form 2D *(continued)*
Page 79

Chapter Test, Form 3
Page 80

Page 81

8. **H**

9. **B**

10. **J**

11. **C**

12. **F**

13. **D**

14. **F**

1. $\dfrac{17}{18}$

2. $\dfrac{7}{9}$

3. $\dfrac{5}{12}$

4. $\dfrac{13}{24}$

5. $31\dfrac{2}{3}$ **pounds**

6. **$15.41**

7. $\dfrac{3}{4}$ **hour**

8. $3 + 1 + 1 = 5$

9. $2 + 10 + 6 = 18$

10. $3\dfrac{3}{8}$

11. $10\dfrac{9}{10}$

12. $2\dfrac{4}{5}$

13. $1\dfrac{7}{9}$

14. $4\dfrac{6}{7}$

Chapter 10 Assessment Answer Key

Page 72, Chapter Extended-Response Test
Scoring Rubric

Level	Specific Criteria
4	The student demonstrates a **_thorough understanding_** of the mathematics concepts and/or procedures embodied in the task. The student has responded correctly to the task, used mathematically sound procedures, and provided clear and complete explanations and interpretations. The response may contain minor flaws that do not detract from the demonstration of a thorough understanding.
3	The student demonstrates an **_understanding_** of the mathematics concepts and/or procedures embodied in the task. The student's response to the task is essentially correct, with the mathematical procedures used and the explanations and interpretations provided demonstrating an essential but less than thorough understanding. The response may contain minor errors that reflect inattentive execution of the mathematical procedures or indications of some misunderstanding of the underlying mathematics concepts and/or procedures.
2	The student has demonstrated only a **_partial understanding_** of the mathematics concepts and/or procedures embodied in the task. Although the student may have used the correct approach to obtaining a solution or may have provided a correct solution, the student's work lacks an essential understanding of the underlying mathematical concepts. The response contains errors related to misunderstanding important aspects of the task, misuse of mathematical procedures, or faulty interpretations of results.
1	The student has demonstrated a **_very limited understanding_** of the mathematics concepts and/or procedures embodied in the task. The student's response to the task is incomplete and exhibits many flaws. Although the student has addressed some of the conditions of the task, the student reached an inadequate conclusion and/or provided reasoning that was faulty or incomplete. The response exhibits many errors or may be incomplete.
0	The student has provided a **_completely incorrect_** solution or uninterpretable response, or no response at all.

Answers

Chapter 10 Assessment Answer Key

In addition to the scoring rubric found on page A30, the following sample answers may be used as guidance in evaluating open-ended assessment items.

1. A fraction is a number that names parts of a whole. $\frac{1}{2}$ is a fraction. This is a drawing of the fraction $\frac{1}{2}$. There are 10 sections and 5 of the sections are shaded in. $\frac{5}{10} = \frac{1}{2}$, so this is a drawing of $\frac{1}{2}$.

2. $\frac{13}{18}$ is still on the tree.

   a. A numerator is the part of the fraction that tells how many of the equal parts are being used. Patrick ate $\frac{3}{18}$ of the apples, so 3 is the numerator. $\frac{2}{18}$ of the apples fell to the ground, so 2 is the numerator.

   b. A denominator is the bottom number in a fraction. In the fraction $\frac{3}{4}$, 4 is the denominator. This means that the object is divided into 4 equal parts. Patrick ate $\frac{3}{18}$ of the apples, so 18 is the denominator. $\frac{2}{18}$ of the apples fell to the ground, so 18 is the denominator.

   c. Patrick ate $\frac{3}{18}$ of the apples, and $\frac{2}{18}$ of the apples fell to the ground. $\frac{3}{18} + \frac{2}{18} = \frac{5}{18}$. So $\frac{5}{18}$ of the apples are no longer on the tree.

3. When a fraction is in simplest form, the numerator and denominator have no common factor greater than 1.

   a. $\frac{1}{5}$

   b. $\frac{1}{5}$

   c. $\frac{1}{3}$

   d. The numerator and denominator of each of the fractions above have no common factor greater than 1.

4. Equivalent fractions are fractions that represent the same number. Patrick climbed the Donaldsons' apple tree and $\frac{9}{18}$ of the apples fell. The next day, Dawn climbed the tree and gathered $\frac{9}{18}$ of the apples. The two amounts represent equivalent fractions. They each represent $\frac{1}{2}$ of the total number of apples.

Chapter 10 Assessment Answer Key

Cumulative Test Practice Chapters 1–10

Page 83   **Page 84**   **Page 85**

3. __B__

8. __G__

9. __$\dfrac{2}{3}$__

4. __H__

10. __$\dfrac{2}{3}$__

11. __$\dfrac{5}{9}$__

5. __A__

12. __$\dfrac{3}{5}$__

6. __H__

13. __$\dfrac{2}{3} > \dfrac{4}{10}$__

1. __B__

14. __$\dfrac{1}{6}$__

2. __J__

7. __B__

Answers